PRAISE FOR IN MY FATHER'S HOUSE

"Growing up in my Father's house was being brought up in a home that mirrored the unconditional love expressed in the Gospel. We always felt secure and wanted, with love equally shared among my siblings. I always appreciated the authenticity and honesty of our lives. Everyone was encouraged to be open and honest to each other as well as our friends and family outside the home. I always felt our private lives compared very similarly to our public lives, which can be difficult in a pastor's home. Most of all, I cherished the equality embodied in our home, between my father and mother as well as between siblings. Everyone was seen as important, valuable, and worthy of time and love."

— AJ Davidiuk
Board Certified Surgeon

When I think back on my time growing up in my father's house, pleasant feelings of nostalgia and many wonderful memories flood my mind. I remember receiving big hugs from my dad when he picked me up from school and being overwhelmed with the comforting smell of his cologne mixed with the scent of the black leather jacket he typically wore. I remember catching ground balls and pop flies from him, playing driveway basketball, and swinging as hard as we could with the persimmon clubs at the driving range and beaming with satisfaction as our skills slowly surpassed his.

I remember basement hockey, hallway soccer, and asking my dad to help me beat the difficult levels on Super Mario Bros. There are many other wonderful memories that I could share with you from my time as a young child and throughout my life into adulthood now with my father. But more important than any of those fun activities is the way my dad made me feel growing up.

As one of the sensitive ones in the family, I'm tearing up a bit as I write this, but it's hard to fully express how much unconditional love there was in our home. I could always go to my father after making a mistake or during times of need. I still can and do. He always knew how to comfort me during these incredibly formative times, and he is the most generous person I have ever met. My father wasn't perfect (no earthly father is), but he showed us how to apologize when he was wrong, and his heart of gold made it difficult to stay mad at him long. He focused on what is important in life and gave me the best example of a father whose love knows no bounds. I love you, Dad, and I will always hold on to the lessons that you taught me.

— Luke J. Davidiuk
Captain, USAF, BSC, PsyD

"Our home was full of so much love, laughter and grace. Something I most admired about my dad is that he always had time to listen and offer an encouraging word. No matter how anxious or worried or afraid I felt, I found comfort in speaking with him. My father's words are like gold to my soul as I always felt he had a direct line to Jesus. The most important thing he showed me was how much value and worth I had as a woman and a daughter of Christ.

My dad always knew what to say to make me feel extra special. Watching the way he loved my mom and seeing how intentional they were about making each other a priority showed me what I wanted and expected out of my own marriage. I'll never forget as a little girl, I'd beg my Dad to lay beside me and read a book until I fell asleep. He gave me the quality time my heart deeply desired. Those are the precious memories I still carry with me. I'm blessed to have him as my dad and a part of my life."

— Larissa Davidiuk Stewart
Stay-at-home mom

While reading my husband's book, I enjoyed re-living those precious moments of parenting our children. This book is so needed at this critical time in history when the nuclear family is being targeted and fathers appear to have become either complacent or absent.

It has been both a joy and an honor parenting our three children with my husband, who I can truly say, was involved in both their physical as well as their spiritual upbringing. I will forever be grateful for the time and investment made in our children's lives.

As you read this book, my prayer is that you receive Godly insights that will help inspire you to be a parent that "blesses his home." Joshua 15:2: "As for me and my Family we will serve the Lord."

— Esty Davidiuk
Registered Nurse Case Manager, retired

For over 50 years, I've seen firsthand the blessing and calling of God on my best friend George's life and ministry, passed on from his father and now passed on to his children and grandchildren. The lessons he has learned along the way are powerfully shared in this book. I highly recommend it to anyone seeking God's calling, direction and encouragement as they take on the wonderful and exciting challenge of being a parent!

— **Paul Chodniewicz,**
CEO of PC Builders and lifelong friend

You have in your hands very useful and practical recommendations from an experienced servant of God who is a kind and loving father and grandfather. Knowing George Davidiuk well as a pastor, teacher, and preacher of the gospel, as well as a good father and family man, I encourage everyone to read this book and practice it in their own lives.

— **Bishop Viktor Limonchenko**
United Slavic Pentecostal Fellowship

George Davidiuk's book, "In My Father's House", is chock full of practical things a father can do to raise spiritually healthy children. I know George well and can say, unequivocally, that he has the authority to write about this subject. If you have ever wondered how to become a better father, read this book!

— **Peter J. Iliyn**
Former North American Director, Youth With A Mission

The art of intergenerational relationships is one of the most common challenges in family relationships today, regardless of culture or continent. For over 30 years, I have been in close relationship with the author's family.

I have had the honor of meeting George's parents in person as a guest staying in their home. Now, as I listen to George's memories of his dad, I'm impressed with George's attitude to his father's contribution to his upbringing. For me, it's a model to emulate.

I have personally observed that the Gospel itself was very much a part of the practical life and faith in the family of George's parents and remains a source of inspiration and counsel in the author's life. I believe that this book will be a great blessing in response to every reader, parent, and family.

— Bishop Viktor Prokhor,
Superintendent of the National Slavic District of the
Assemblies of God
Pastor of Life Christian Church, Tacoma, WA

In My Father's House

HOW TO BE A DAD
WHO BLESSES HIS HOME

GEORGE DAVIDIUK

Fedd Books
P.O. Box 341973
Austin, TX 78734
www.thefeddagency.com

Published in association with The Fedd Agency, Inc., a literary agency.

Any words in bold in the Bible verses or quotes are added by the author for emphasis.

ISBN: 978-1-949784-50-3
eISBN: 978-1-949784-51-0
Library of Congress Control Number: 2020918453

Printed in the United States of America

First Edition 20 21 22 23 / 5 4 3 2 1

To my Tato, my kind, immigrant father who was such a great example of a faithful father and a man of God. You showed me a glimpse of what our heavenly Father is like. I miss you.

Table of Contents

Preface.. 15

Introduction:
The Prodigal Son and the Father 17

Chapter 1:
In My Father's House.. 23

Chapter 2:
In My Earthly Father's House 27

Chapter 3:
Healthy Boundaries.. 35

Chapter 4:
Godly Discipline 41

Chapter 5:
Consequences: Luke's Bubbles and AJ's Ball 55

Chapter 6:
When Should I Have "That Talk" with My Children? 63

Chapter 7:
Vision, Direction, and Identity 69

Chapter 8:
Childhood Training.. 83

Chapter 9:
How Do I Protect My Family? Part 1 93

Chapter 10:
How Do I Protect My Family? Part 2 103

Chapter 11:
Battling and Overcoming Addiction 113

Chapter 12:
The Power of Encouragement 123

Chapter 13:
Asking Forgiveness: Passwords, Pride, and Patience 135

Chapter 14:
Being Honest: The Christmas Chairs.. 139

Chapter 15:
The Best Dad in the Bible.. 145

Chapter 16:
The Privilege to Bless 183

Chapter 17:
Releasing Your Children.. 191

Chapter 18:
Returning Home 201

Preface

My objective for this book is to illustrate the powerful influence that a father has in his family. This book is for men, whether they are fathers, sons, or big brothers who are helping their single mothers because their own fathers are absent.

It will become quite obvious that I am not an expert here. Far from it! Rather than provide you with scientific data or informational results of surveys and tests, my simple goal is to share with you my own experiences and memories as a son and as a father. My desire is for you to be, by the grace of God, the best father you can be. That is what I try to be.

So many books on parenting have been written specifically for mothers. It is much easier to recognize the traditional role that a mother has with her children. She carries the unborn infant in her womb, labors through his birth, feeds him at her breast, and nurtures him through the most helpless and vulnerable period of his life. She is fiercely protective of his childhood, and she hovers nearby as he takes his first faltering steps. But what about the father? What is he expected to do?

Too often the father is content to withdraw into the comfortable role of his work, relegating the education and child-raising to the mother. After all, in many cases he is the provider, working hard outside the home to provide the necessities and the luxuries for his family. The mom raises the kids, and the dad brings home the bacon (or for Slavic people, the *kovbasa*!), right?

That is all good, but sometimes the father can fail to recognize the tremendous responsibility God calls him to fulfill. God has designed the father to have the role of being actively and intimately involved in the care and protection of his sons and daughters, and to help teach them the lessons of life. Raising children is not just the mother's responsibility, as is so often assumed in our culture. That is what this book is about.

So, moms, I hope you don't feel left out that I am writing this book for men. They just need a book like this more than you do—but I don't mind if you read it. In fact, buy it for your husband!

INTRODUCTION:

The Prodigal Son and the Father

The hunger in Demas's stomach gnawed at him. He was so hungry that it felt as if mice were chewing on his insides.

What am I doing here? he questioned, anger welling up inside him as he stood knee-deep in the slippery mud of the filthy pigpen, watching pigs fight over the last few cornhusks.

Pigs! he thought. *If only my father could see me now—a Jewish boy raised on his wealthy father's farm, stuck in this stinking mud with pigs. With pigs! Not kosher, not kosher at all!*

That thought brought him deep shame and overwhelmed him with a sense of failure. *How did I end up here?* His thoughts went back to the young toughs from the village pub: "C'mon! Join us, and we'll party! We know some loose women!"

Yeah, loose women! Most likely they were the reason that the money he begged his father to give him as his early inheritance disappeared faster than the dew on a hot summer morning.

And why was I the only one paying for everything? he lamented, recalling how more and more people he didn't even know joined his parties. *Now my money is all gone, and what am I left with? A miserable job tending stinking pigs!*

His thoughts drifted back to his father's house. *Home,* he thought, longingly remembering the farm his father had painstakingly built on a huge plot of land in the lush, fertile hills of the Judean countryside. Thoughts of his mother baking fresh, warm bread triggered his senses and intensified his hunger pangs. He recalled their family dinner table overloaded with fresh vegetables from the garden, and his favorite dish—grilled lamb roasted over hot charcoals, dripping with savory juices. He thought of the many servants scurrying about their household tasks and bringing full trays of exotic fruits for dessert.

Servants! In my father's house, even the lowest servants ate better than I am eating now. They got to choose from the leftovers of our household meals, and here I am, starving in this pig pen! Why had he left such a warm and comfortable home to chase elusive pleasures in this distant land?

Could I possibly go back? he wondered. *Would my*

father take me on as a servant? Even as his servant, I would still be much better off than I am now!

Jesus tells this gripping parable in Luke 15. It is the story of how the poor life choices of this young man drove him from a place of privilege to a pit of despair. Yet Jesus goes on to tell us that the young man deeply repented before God, and when he made his way back to his father's house, his father fully restored him as his son.

What is the central truth of this parable? Who is the story really about? Is it about the lost son, or is it about the kind and loving father who tearfully welcomed his son home and joyfully celebrated his return, not just with a simple dinner, but with a feast?

What motivated the boy to return home? Was it because he had run out of money? Was it because he was hungry and cold? Was it the horrible circumstances that he found himself in, living among pigs—an animal forbidden in his strict Jewish culture? Certainly these were all important and motivating factors, but the greatest reason and the heart of the teaching of Jesus was that it was the warm memory of his father's house that drove this wayward son to rise up and walk barefoot the long distance back home. The young man realized that even a life as a servant in his father's house would be better than the life he found himself living among pigs. What he did not realize was that his loving father would forgive him, receive him as his son (rather than as a servant), and celebrate his return home with a feast.

As Jesus relates this story, a picture emerges of a watchful, hopeful father who is so elated when his son finally returns home that all work stops and a happy celebration follows. Like this earthly father, God, as our heavenly Father, yearns for His children to be with Him in the home He has prepared for them.

Jesus tells us: "In My Father's house are many mansions" (John 14:2 NKJV). Jesus wants His disciples and followers to know that His heavenly Father has prepared a place for them, His children, to be with Him for eternity.

The parable of the prodigal son, along with this passage from John, became my inspiration to write this book and expand on what the phrase "in My Father's house" means for me, while also exploring what it can mean for you. My goal is to motivate men to be better fathers to their children. I want you to create such wonderful memories together that your children will always long to return to a home they remember as a place of warmth and love and as a wonderful celebration of family.

We will return to the Luke 15 story of the prodigal son and his father later and will delve deeper into the character of this father and his relationship with his son. In the meantime, let's jump into your relationship with your children. What would your children say about their childhood memories or about growing up in their father's house? As you read this book, I hope you will be inspired to be like the father in Jesus's parable of the prodigal son and that you will make your home a place of blessing!

CHAPTER 1:

In My Father's House

"In My Father's house." These words spoken by Jesus in John 14 hold immense meaning for me on a personal level. I have wonderful memories of my earthly father's house, and my childhood was truly memorable because my father created such a pleasant and warm atmosphere in our home. He was a very kind man, and his heart and sincere love for God brought much blessing and security to our family. From childhood through early adulthood, I learned many valuable lessons living in my father's house. I want to share some of those lessons with you.

Jesus often described His heavenly Father and spoke of their close relationship. Even at the age of twelve, when His parents, Joseph and Mary, thought He was missing and frantically searched for Him, eventually finding Him at the temple, Jesus asked them, "Didn't you know I had to be **in my Father's house?**" (Luke 2:49 NIV). Later, when Jesus was concluding His earthly ministry and spoke of

His ascension, He comforted His anxious disciples with these words: "Let not your heart be troubled. . . . **In My Father's house** are many mansions" (John 14:1–2 NKJV).

Jesus also gave an incredible description of the character of His heavenly Father in Luke 15, where He tells the story of a father whose son leaves home. In this parable, the parable of the prodigal son, Jesus reveals that this lost young man returned to his father's house because it was a place of acceptance, forgiveness, and love. Of all the parables Jesus tells, this story of a forgiving father best reveals the heart of God the Father. It tells about His character, that He receives sinners, and that He greatly desires to forgive us and then celebrate together.

We usually hear this story told from the perspective of the lost son. This book's introduction does just that. However, when I began to meditate on Jesus's description of the father of this wayward son, it struck me how wonderful a father he was. Chapter 15 of this book discusses eight lessons we can learn from this father.

God has placed on my heart a deep desire to encourage fathers—especially among the Slavic community that I serve—to follow this amazing example of a father, given to us by Jesus, so that we would become even better fathers ourselves. We should make our homes places that our children will always want to return to in times of need.

My greatest desire for you dear fathers who read

this book is that your children would say of you, "My father's house is a place of acceptance, forgiveness, and unconditional love." This is what our children desire even more than all the material things we could ever give them.

Our kids don't need more toys from us; their hearts cry out **for us**. They want us to spend more time with them. You might be surprised to hear that, just as I was. This revelation came to me as an answer to a simple question I asked on social media.

A while back, I took an informal, one-question survey of the readers of my public Facebook page. I asked: **"What, in your opinion, is the greatest need in Slavic churches today?"**

The responses really surprised me! Of the more than eight thousand followers of this page (at that time), 72 percent were between the ages of thirteen to thirty-four, and 28 percent were thirty-five and older.

As I began to tally the different answers into the top three categories, my initial thought was that the number-one response would be for more English to be used in Slavic churches. However, that ranked as the number-three response. The number-two response also surprised me: "I wish my pastor would prepare better sermons!" Wow! That challenges us preachers to become better communicators of God's Word!

What do you think the number-one response was? The number-one response was: **"I wish my father spent**

more time with me!"

Take notice, dear men; this is the cry of the hearts of our sons and daughters: **more time** with their dads.

It is understandable when a father's work takes him away from his family for brief periods of time. Nevertheless, the question is not about what we can do for our children while we are away, but about what we can do for them when we are at **home.**

Do we pursue our own interests as men and leave the upbringing of our children to their mother, or are we willing to sacrifice ourselves and our interests and invest in the lives of our sons and daughters, who are greatly affected by our behavior and choices? This is a choice that we all must make as fathers.

Fathers, my prayer is that as you read this book, you will be inspired to find ways to spend time with your families, especially with your children—as they grow up **in their father's house.**

CHAPTER 2:

In My Earthly Father's House

At this time Moses was born; and he was beautiful in
God's sight. And he was brought up for three months in
his father's house.
Acts 7:20 ESV

Let me ask you a question: What kind of home were you raised in? What was **your** father's house like? Let me begin by telling you about my father's house. It might not be typical, but I was blessed with a very kind and loving father.

My earthly father's house was warm and loving, even though it was very humble. My parents immigrated to the United States in 1950 before I was born. Fleeing the Soviet Union, and then war-torn Germany, they arrived at Ellis Island in New York Harbor with my two older sisters, Rosita, aged five, and Helen, aged three. I was born four years later, in 1954, in Newark, New Jersey, eighteen miles away from New York City.

My parents had three more children born to them after me—a set of fraternal girl twins whom they named Ruth and Joyce, and the last-born girl named Joy. Tragically, Joyce died in my father's arms of a perforated septum in her heart at the age of eleven months. However, this was not the first time one of my parents' children had died. Their firstborn baby, a boy whom they also named George, was born in Western Ukraine, and he went to be with Jesus only a day after his birth.

Both of my parents knew the horror of World War II, the tyranny of Communism, and the tragedy of the death of a beloved child. It was why they so much loved coming to a free country like America.

A kind pastor by the name of Fred Smolchuck had sponsored my parents' immigration to this country, and he offered Dad the pastorate of a small congregation of Ukrainian immigrants in Newark. The congregation consisted of about eleven members—nine elderly women and two men. It would grow to become a very large church filled with young people.

We moved to a home in the neighboring town of Irvington that was only half a block away from the church. We lived in the first-floor apartment of a six-family house. The apartment consisted of four rooms that were heated by kerosene that Dad brought in from a big round metal storage tank in our backyard.

Dad never learned to drive, so he never owned a car. That sounds strange, doesn't it? I was born and raised in America, and we had to take a bus everywhere until I got my driver's license at the age of seventeen!

Memories of My Father

I remember my father taking me to church with him for Wednesday night prayer meetings before I was even old enough to go to school. He would bribe me by promising to take me out for ice cream afterward, and as a result, I never missed a Wednesday night prayer meeting.

Although Dad was the pastor of a growing church for so many people, to me he was always still my father. At bedtime, he always had time to tell me a story, usually about a *syritka* (an orphan child). Then he prayed with me. Every day. No kidding. My father prayed with me every single day that I can remember.

Before taking me to my first day of kindergarten at Grove Street School in Irvington, my father and I stopped at our front door and prayed. This continued throughout my years in elementary school, and then all throughout my high school years.

Although he didn't make much money as the pastor of the Ukrainian Evangelical Assemblies of God Church, I remember the first bicycle he bought me. It was red and had one speed—"pedal fast!" He bought it on credit and then paid it off by sending me to the storeowner once a week with five dollars in quarters.

Our home always had good food on the table and lots of guests. As my father was the pastor of our church, these guests were usually visiting ministers. They always had great stories to tell a young boy who was growing up in a pastor's house, and they would often stay in our house. Our home was small, so I would often have to sleep on the couch in the living room so that our guest could sleep in my bedroom.

One Saturday night I attended a wedding in another town. I was only sixteen or seventeen years old at the time and had to wait for my friends to drive me home. The wedding finished very late, and by the time I arrived home, I could see that the windows of our house were all dark; everyone was sleeping. My mom had locked the front door for the night, and I discovered that I didn't have a key with me.

No problem, I thought. *I can climb in through my bedroom window at the back of our house.* I always kept my bedroom window unlocked for just that purpose.

As I slowly squeezed my body through the window frame, I looked to my bed and saw a man sleeping there! *Oh no! It must be a visiting preacher!* I thought.

What do I do now? I wondered, half hanging into my room and half dangling outside. *If I back out and go to the front door, I will still have to ring the doorbell and wake everybody up. I am halfway in, so maybe I can quietly squeeze myself the rest of the way in.*

Just then, the preacher woke up and saw me hanging halfway in the window of the room he was sleeping in.

"Who arr you? Vat do you vant?" he exclaimed in broken English.

"It's okay!" I attempted to explain. "I am Pastor Davidiuk's son, and I had no key to the front door. I didn't know you were sleeping in my bed."

The visitor took a breath to calm his thumping heart, and then he said, "Don't vorry, I no tell your father." I just shook my head and headed for the couch in the living room.

Unlike other teenage boys who might not want to tell their fathers that they were caught climbing through a window in the middle of the night, I wasn't afraid to tell Dad the next morning what had happened. He laughed when I told him of our startled guest's reaction.

When I think of that episode now, I laugh quietly to myself. What must it have looked like for that visiting preacher to wake up from sleeping soundly and see a stranger climbing through his window? Memories like these were made in my home.

There is a deeper lesson from that humorous episode, though. My father raised me with grace instead of with law. He trusted me to do the right thing when I was out with my friends. My father's trust in me truly made me not want to sin and hurt him in any way.

My father's house is where I learned some of the

greatest lessons of my life.

Fathers, take advantage of every moment with your child while they are still living with you in your home. Use everyday occurrences as teaching moments. After your son or daughter is grown up, those lessons they learned in their father's house will remain with them.

Dad passed away in 1996 at the age of eighty-five, but I can never forget his teachings—pearls of wisdom that he passed on to me.

When I was just beginning in ministry and was starting to preach my first stumbling sermons, some of the sermons did not turn out very well. My father saw that I was unsure of myself while preaching, and he encouraged me: "Son, you must preach as if your message is the most important thing you could ever tell anyone!"

When my spiritual life would sometimes cool off, he would always notice. He would lift up my faltering heart by saying, "Son, always seek to be filled with God's Spirit!"

When he noticed that I had discovered girls, he prepared me: "Keep yourself pure for marriage, Son. I did, and you can too." He then told me very revealing personal stories that stayed with me. He surprised me with his honesty and willingness to share intimate moments. I later passed those stories about my dad to my own boys. Their reaction: "Dido (Grandfather)? No way! That really happened?" (I'll tell you the unforgettable story that elicited that reaction later on in this book.)

It was my father who taught me to live by faith, always trusting God. His example of simple faith and trust in God was very evident in our home, and it powerfully affected my own faith. He was the one who told me again and again that God had a destiny for me and a unique calling on my life.

My Father's Greatest Legacy

A legacy is something that a person leaves behind to be remembered by. It could be money or land or a house inherited from your parents—but in my case, it was something far more valuable.

My father, Andrew Davidiuk, left behind a legacy of prayer for his family. Often when I entered his office in our home (which also served as my bedroom), he would be on his knees praying for our family and for the church he pastored. Those prayers that my father prayed for my life and ministry became my greatest and richest inheritance. His example of praying on his knees left an indelible mark on my young life as I grew up in his house.

Dear fathers, what legacy will you leave for your children as they grow up in your home?

CHAPTER 3:

Healthy Boundaries

*Set up road **markers** for yourself; make yourself **guideposts**;*
*consider well the highway, the **road** by which you went.*
Jeremiah 31:21 ESV

"It's time!" your wife anxiously tells you. "Take me to the hospital. The baby is coming! NOW!"

For my wife and me, it was two o'clock in the morning when our first baby boy decided to announce his arrival. We lived in Franklin Park, New Jersey, at the time, and we drove the forty-five-minute-route to St. Barnabas Hospital in Livingston, New Jersey, in twenty minutes. My wife, Esty, worked as a nurse in the OB-GYN floor, and her fellow nurses were waiting for us. After long, arduous labor, my wife delivered our first baby.

After waiting nine months for this momentous event, we held this bundle of joy in our arms. A few days into being a father, as my wife and all the women in my family gushed about how cute he was, I took a good look and wondered, *I am not so sure about that. No hair, no teeth, and he doesn't even talk yet! He just sleeps all day, cries all night, and wants to eat all the time! Worse yet, he goes through ten diapers a day. This is getting expensive!*

To be honest, it will seem to most fathers as if this is Mommy's time with the baby. She feeds him, holds him, and rocks him to sleep. Most fathers can't wait for the time when they can interact with the baby by more than just holding and rocking him. They look forward to throwing the ball together, running in the park together, and actually having a conversation!

Those days will come. Eventually your sweet little baby begins to repeat what he or she hears you say. At first, the words are simple, usually Ma-Ma or Da-Da. It's really exciting to hear your child's first feeble attempts at communication. They are actually talking!

Yet as they quickly grow and develop, you will soon hear them say that small little word—"No!"

"Eat your vegetables."

"No!"

"Share your toy with your friend."

"No!"

Now what? This baby is not so cute anymore!

On one hand, this is pretty normal behavior. The child is testing the parents to see what he can get away with. In other words, he is learning where the boundaries are.

What is a **boundary**? It is a line that determines the **limits** of something. Countries have boundaries, or borders. Every piece of property has a boundary that determines its limits.

Children must learn their boundaries as well. This is very important to their healthy development, both with others and with themselves. When a child doesn't know his boundaries or limits, he begins to feel very insecure.

The next time your infant is asleep in his crib or bed, notice that he never sleeps in the middle of the mattress. He is always tucked up against one of the sides of the crib or almost on the edge of the mattress. Why is this? He needs to know where the bed ends. This actually brings comfort. The child thinks, *This is how big my bed is. I know my bed.*

This is also true with boundaries regarding a child's behavior. As parents, it is our job—it is our **responsibility**—to teach our growing children where their boundaries are. It is our responsibility to teach our children what behavior is acceptable and what behavior is not. The Bible admonishes us: "Train up a child in the way he should go, even when he is old, he will not depart from it" (Proverbs 22:6 NASB).

When your child says "No!" to you or deliberately disobeys you, he then watches closely to see how you are going to react. Please don't say, "Oh, how cute! He's feisty!" This response will only encourage them to continue their selfish behavior. You must act decisively and consistently as you train your child to obey your authority. If you do not, your child will only push the boundaries of selfish behavior further and further until there are no longer any limits.

In his classic book *Dare to Discipline,* Dr. James Dobson tells of a conversation he had with a mother whose teenager became a juvenile delinquent and ended up in jail. Dobson asked her, "When did you first realize that you lost authority over your boy?" She responded that she remembers the exact day. Dobson writes:

> Her son was less than three at the time. She carried him to his room and placed him in his crib, and he spit in her face. She explained the importance of not spitting in mommy's face, but was interrupted by another moist missile. This mother had been told that all confrontations could be resolved by love, understanding, and discussion. So she wiped her face and began again, at which point she was hit with another well-aimed blast. Growing increasingly frustrated, she shook him . . . but not hard enough to disrupt his aim with the next wad.
>
> What could she do then? Her philosophy offered no honorable solution to this embarrassing challenge. Finally, she rushed from the room in

utter exasperation, and her little conqueror spat on the back of the door as it shut.

She lost; he won! This exasperated mother told me she never had the upper hand with her child after that night![1]

When parents lose these early confrontations with their children, it becomes much harder later on to win the child's respect and obedience. If you cannot make a five-year-old pick up his toys, then it's not likely you will have much influence on him when he is in his turbulent teenage years.

The question, then, is how do we teach our young children obedience so that they grow up to respect authority in their lives?

Read on, brave parent.

CHAPTER 4:

Godly Discipline

A refusal to correct is a refusal to love;
*love your children by **disciplining** them.*
Proverbs 13:24 MSG

One of the most difficult parts of parenting is administering proper and loving discipline to your children, yet the Bible clearly teaches the importance of **correct** discipline in shaping the character of a child.

In the previous chapter, we spoke of the need to teach healthy boundaries to our children. These boundaries provide safety to a child, much like the guardrails on the sides of a narrow mountain highway prevent you from driving your car off the edge of the cliff. Boundaries and guardrails keep us from danger.

A lack of boundaries, or guardrails, in our lives can lead us to drive off the road to our spiritual, or even physical, deaths.

The goal of discipline is not to produce perfect kids,

but rather to protect them from dangerous attitudes and activities that can greatly harm them. By nature, children can be stubborn, selfish, lazy, and disrespectful—just like us adults. Such is the nature of humanity in a sinful world. How do we help our children to overcome these sinful traits as they grow up?

The first step is to patiently teach them that there are consequences for disobedience and rewards for obedience. Children quickly learn what they are allowed to do and what they are not allowed to do. Godly discipline begins in their early years and reinforces those lessons.

Let me share with you some practical tips regarding discipline that we implemented with our children.

Inform Adequately

In our home, we did not have a lot of rules, but we had a few very important ones. Respect for parents and older people, church attendance and prayer, and doing homework and getting good grades were among those important matters.

I learned from my own father not to major in the minors. When we discipline a child for every little thing, the battles over the less important issues will distract a child from the major issues of life. With children, picking your battles is a very important principle. Fight for the values that are the most important in your child's heart.

Once you recognize and define the values that are important for your family, inform your children adequately as to what is expected of them. Make the rules clear and easy to understand. You will have to repeat them often and will need to give your children sufficient warning of the consequences of breaking these rules. It is easier for children to understand what is expected from them when it is spelled out in black and white.

Avoid Extremes of Discipline

One mistake of fearful parents is to severely **restrict the freedom** of a growing child. This results in the child wanting to escape the confines of their "jail," and they will fly away from you at their first opportunity. In contrast, when you give your children increased responsibilities and trust as they grow up, they will spread their wings but will always want to fly close to your home. Even if their life vocations take them geographically far from your home, as happened with two of our three children, their hearts will long to be near you as much as is possible.

The other extreme is to allow the child **too much freedom** too early. This can lead the child to disrespect the authority of the parent, and later, any other authority figure, whether that is their teacher, their employer, or a police officer. Trouble awaits those kids who have no rules or who never learned to obey authority figures.

Never Discipline in Anger

One of the biggest mistakes you can make as a parent is to lose your temper with your children. I admit that it is very easy to do when the kids break your favorite radio, lamp, or precious possession. Let's be honest—it provokes us to anger to see our cherished items broken, and it is intuitive to lash out in anger when that happens. We told our children to be careful and not to play ball where Mom has some nice things displayed.

To avoid disciplining my children in anger, I slowly and deliberately counted from one to ten before I administered any kind of discipline. This gave time for my anger to subside. I wanted my child to see the lesson that followed their disobedience rather than seeing my anger. This also gave me an opportunity to speak to their conscience.

Our two boys, Andrew (whom we call AJ) and Luke, must have been about eight and six years old when an incident occurred in which they not only broke our rules, but they damaged a valued painting. Once a month I would take my wife out for dinner on a date night. We asked a babysitter to look after our boys and our three-year-old daughter, Larissa.

When we returned home that evening, all three

children were sweetly sleeping, so we paid the sitter and got ready for bed. When I went to shut the living room lights off, I noticed a hole in my favorite painting that hung above the couch. It was a beautiful painting of a sailboat with bright moonlight reflecting on the water—and it now had a small ball-sized hole in it.

The next morning, I gathered my two boys by the couch and pointed to the painting.

"Anybody care to explain how that hole got there?" I asked. The boys just shrugged their shoulders and tried to act like they had never seen that hole before.

"Oh, so it just appeared magically by itself then?" AJ and Luke probably hoped that I believed that. "Did you throw the ball in the living room?" I continued, with a serious look on my face.

Then the excuses started. One of the boys said, "I didn't throw it; he did!"

"Yeah, but you were supposed to catch it!" answered the other.

"How could I, when you threw it off to the side?" answered the first.

I quickly interrupted and asked in a low and menacing voice, "What did Daddy say?"

"Not to throw the ball in the living room," was the quiet response.

To help them understand things from a parent's perspective, I asked, "Okay, what does Daddy have to do now?"

"Forgive us?" one of them asked hopefully.

"Yes, I could forgive you," I continued, "but then you will just continue to ignore my rule and throw the ball in here again. So my job is to help you remember not to throw a ball in the living room again."

Before I get to what happened next, let's look at three more important tips about discipline.

Appeal to Their Conscience

One of the greatest lessons we can teach our children is why their action or disobedience was wrong. The heart is the best motivator for doing the right thing. Whenever any of my children broke one of our rules, I would ask them, "What did Daddy tell you?" or "Is that the right thing to do?"

A tender conscience is of great value in a child because we live in a sinful and careless world that tends to disregard all laws and respect for authority. It is of the utmost importance that we let our children know that God has told us in His Word, the Bible, that parents are to discipline their children. We must obey God, and we must teach our children to do the same.

It is not just **our** rule, but it is also **God's** rule.

Avoid Nagging or Making Empty Threats

Have you noticed that some parents have to tell their children the same thing four or five times to get them to obey? Don't blame the kids when this happens; the parents are the ones who are actually producing this result. For example, consider the following common scenario:

A parent tells a child, "Pick up your toys and get ready for a bath." The child ignores the parent, who patiently repeats the request.

"Come on! I told you to pick up your toys. Let's go!" Of course, this time it is spoken a little louder, but still—no results. The child calmly continues to play.

"What did I say?" yells the exasperated parent, but the child knows that the boiling point has not yet been reached.

Finally, the parent jerks the child up by the arm and yells, "I told you to pick up your toys and get ready for a bath!"

The child has figured out that it takes at least four verbal repetitions before the parent takes action.

Nagging your child—repeating your words to someone who ignores you while you continue to expect a different result—does not work; it is very ineffective. Dr. James Dobson in *Dare to Discipline* says it well: "Trying to control your children by screaming at them is as futile as trying to steer a car by honking the horn." If there is no first-time obedience (or at most, just one reminder), then some measure of discipline is called for, such as a "time out" or making the child stand in a corner.

Do not threaten punishment unless you are ready to follow through. The child quickly learns whether you mean what you say or not. You don't need to say it four times to get results.

Discern Whether to Use Concrete or Abstract Discipline

It is critical to recognize that the different stages of a child's growing years require different methods of discipline that a parent can use to mold their child's behavior most effectively.

From birth to about four years of age, the little infants and toddlers cannot yet make decisions for themselves. The parents will choose what the children eat and when they sleep. These are **concrete** choices all made by the parent. On the other hand, **abstract** choices give the child a measure of freedom to make their own decisions, and this freedom of choice should gradually increase as the child grows older and matures.

Our goal as parents is to prepare our children for the turbulent teenage years and to bring them to maturity as adults. This calls for a wise balance of concrete and abstract choices as they are growing up. To put it another way, we do not want to clip our children's wings so that they never fly, but we want to give our children wings so they can soar higher and achieve wonderful things.

When a toddler deliberately and willfully refuses to obey a parent, some explanation of the poor behavior is needed, but words will not be enough for a child this young. Physical discipline of some kind is needed as a painful consequence. In today's permissive society, that sounds very violent.

Let's return to our story and examine the subject of spanking. Proverbs, the book of wisdom, tells us, "Whoever spares **the rod** hates his son, but he who loves him is **diligent** to **discipline** him" (Proverbs 13:24 ESV). The Bible speaks of using physical punishment as a form of discipline for a child, and I believe that this is effective for rare use in cases of direct and willful disobedience. Even then, there is a proper way of doing it so we don't discourage our children or provoke them to anger, as Ephesians 6:4 says.

Let's review our checklist of the principles we have discussed:

- Inform adequately so your child knows the rules.
- Avoid the extremes of discipline.
- Let your anger cool down.
- Speak to the conscience of your child.
- Avoid nagging and empty words, and follow through with consequences.

- Discern whether to use concrete or abstract discipline with your child.

There will come a time when **only** spanking your children will teach them to respect your authority and obey the rules of your family.

"Do you mean I have to physically hit my child for disobeying me? Won't that teach him violence?" ask some concerned parents.

The answer is no, it won't teach him violence, and this is why. The best lessons in life are sometimes learned negatively. We are told not to touch a hot stove, but curiosity makes us do it. "Ouch! It hurts!" Yes, and because it hurts, we learn not to touch it again.

"Don't pull on the tablecloth!" But it is so tempting to pull it—and bang! The vase hits us on the nose. No more pulling the tablecloth. Do these lessons cause us to become violent? No. These tough lessons teach us that it is better not to do those specific things because hurt will inevitably follow. "Do not withhold discipline from a child; if you strike him with a rod, **he will not die**" (Proverbs 23:13 ESV).

Always Use a Neutral Object for Spanking

Now back to our story of the painting with a hole.

"Okay, boys, Daddy will have to give you three 'hot

ones' for disobeying his instructions." I would always tell my children in advance what the amount of punishment would be.

I would take my children into the bedroom separately. There is no need to embarrass them in front of each other. A neutral object works best, such as a belt or a large spoon, to administer the spanking. I would discourage using your hand to spank, as your hands should be used for gestures of affection with your children.

"Turn over, son, and lie on your stomach." The best place to receive these strokes is on the soft, round part of the anatomy, and always with the pants on. Don't embarrass them by pulling their pants down.

AJ would accept his punishment without arguing. He was the firstborn and was usually compliant with obeying rules and receiving consequences.

My second-born son, Luke, though, would act as the lawyer.

"Wait, Dad. Lemme explain. I told AJ not to throw it, but he threw it anyway. I couldn't catch it because he was off on his throw. We didn't mean to do it, Dad."

"Are you finished, Luke?"

"Yes."

"Okay," I answered. "Now turn over."

"WAIT, Dad! There's more!" Luke would go on to explain further how this was all a terrible mistake and that they wouldn't do it anymore.

"I hear you, Luke. Are you done now? Turn over."

One, two, and three strokes of my belt would hit their buttocks, but never too hard—just enough to sting through their clothes. I do suspect that on at least one occasion Luke stuck a lot of toilet paper under his pants, because his cries of pain sounded very fake.

Always Love and Comfort Immediately After

After giving the spanking, I would never leave the room right away. The child would cry softly, and after giving them a moment, I would always reach out, hold them in my arms, and tell them how much I loved them. They always hugged me back, and our bond grew closer. It might seem strange, but the best communication between parent and child comes after a disciplinary event.

What Lessons Did They Learn?

This is also the best time to ask the child what he learned from this situation. It is a good teaching moment. Let the child tell you what he learned in his own words.

Let me conclude this chapter by saying that whatever method you decide to use in disciplining your children, please remember that your goal should never be to hurt, abuse, or dominate them. Your goal should be to teach them healthy respect for you and for other authority figures they will encounter in life.

For more detailed information on this subject, I highly recommend two of Dr. James Dobson's books on raising well-adjusted children: *Dare to Discipline* and *The Strong-Willed Child*.

CHAPTER 5:

Consequences: Luke's Bubbles and AJ's Ball

Now all discipline seems painful at the time, not joyful. But later it produces the fruit of peace and righteousness for those trained by it.
Hebrews 12:11 NET

Teaching Moments

Fathers, there are a whole lot of teaching moments that come along when our children are little. Yet fathers who might not be very verbal or who do not see themselves as teachers all tend to say the same thing: "I am not good with words. I don't know what to say to my kids. Let their mother handle that."

My response? You don't have to be a skilled speaker to teach your children important life lessons. Situations will arise where your child does something wrong and some kind of discipline is required, and appropriate consequences will remind the child not to repeat that behavior again—but don't stop there! The moments following the discipline are excellent opportunities to talk with your child about what happened, why it was wrong, and how he can do better in the future.

Many of the parables of Jesus were likely told to the disciples as they happened. I am only guessing, but it is not unrealistic to assume that the "Parable of the Sower" was spoken after the disciples witnessed a farmer scattering seed in a field, or that Jesus told the "Parable of the Workers in the Vineyard" as they walked past rows and rows of grapes. The same principle is true when we are raising our children. Many significant events in the lives of our children can serve as excellent, life-changing teaching moments.

In the previous chapter, we discussed some different kinds of discipline that can help teach our children to respect authority. We mentioned physical spanking for the most serious of cases, but there are often other creative ways we can use to convey life lessons to our children. Let me illustrate by sharing two very different examples from the lives of our sons.

Of our two boys, AJ was more of a rule follower, but Luke was more like his father—talkative and sometimes argumentative.

On one occasion when Luke crossed the line and

disrespected me with his words (it couldn't have been that bad because I can't remember the specifics now!), I decided to take an unusual approach. We were in the kitchen and my back was against the sink.

"Luke, if you say that one more time with that attitude of disrespect, I will wash your mouth out with soap!" I threatened.

Evidently, his curiosity got the better of him. *Is Dad really gonna do that?* So he repeated his words, watching my reaction closely. He didn't notice that my hand was behind my back and I had pressed a dollop of dishwashing liquid onto my fingers.

"That is so disrespectful!" I said. "Stick out your tongue!" To my amazement, he did! In a flash, I quickly swiped my soap-covered fingers onto his stuck-out tongue.

What happened next was hilarious. He began to blow bubbles out of his mouth and said, "I can't believe that you did that, Dad!" He had to rinse his mouth out for quite a while because that stuff was so concentrated.

Needless to say, Luke did not use disrespectful words with me after that teaching moment! He learned that there are consequences for disrespectful behavior.

The other teaching moment affected the course of my oldest son's life forever. AJ must have been around five or six years old when he approached me with the news that he needed to buy a birthday present for his school friend Charlie. After all, he was invited to

Charlie's birthday party, and it just wasn't right to show up without a present.

"Let's go to the mega toy store to buy Charlie a birthday present," I said. Knowing that this particular store was toy heaven for a little boy, I saw this as an excellent opportunity to teach my son about unselfishness. "But, AJ," I added, "if we go to that store, it's only to buy a birthday gift for Charlie, okay? Not a toy for you this time."

"Sure, Dad," he replied. At home, it seemed to be such an easy lesson. At the store, with so many delightful temptations for a little boy, it would prove to be a different story.

At the store, we went searching for the perfect birthday gift for Charlie. AJ disappeared for a moment, but he soon came back clutching a pink rubber ball. "Dad, can I get this ball too? It's only a dollar! Look how high it bounces!"

"What's a dollar," I thought. All three of my children love sports. They never asked for much, knowing our money was limited, so a small ball was something I could afford to get him; but we had agreed about learning a lesson of unselfishness. It wasn't really a question of money, but was a matter of principle.

"I'm sorry, Son," I said. "Put it back. We agreed that today we would only buy something for Charlie, right? I'll buy you a ball next time."

AJ reluctantly put the ball back (at least I thought

he did!), and we finished our shopping. As we drove home, the bag with Charlie's gift was on the floor of the car by AJ's feet. Just as we pulled into our driveway, the stopping motion of the car caused a pink ball to roll out of the bag.

AJ watched it roll out with a panicked look on his face. He looked up at me to see if I saw it, looked down at the ball again, and then said with a huge smile, "Wow, Dad! Look at that!" as if the ball had magically appeared in his bag by itself.

To tell you the truth, it was funny to see how quickly he tried to look surprised. I had to bite my lip to stop from laughing out loud, but I said to him in my sternest voice, "You stole that ball, didn't you?"

He looked scared and asked, "Are you going to spank me?"

"No, Son." I replied.

"Oh, thanks, Dad!" he sighed, visibly relieved.

"We are driving back to the store, and you will give the ball back and ask for forgiveness for stealing it."

"Nooooooo!" cried AJ. "Spank me instead! Please don't embarrass me!" he begged all the way back to the store.

"Son, you will learn a difficult, but valuable, lesson by going back and asking for forgiveness. I know that it will help you to never steal anything again."

Part of asking for forgiveness is asking properly. So many people use the word "sorry" that, unfortunately, that overused word has lost its power to elicit true forgiveness from the offended party. So I taught AJ to ask for forgiveness by using the following sentences as he gave the ball back: "God has convicted me of stealing. Would you please forgive me?"

We entered the store again—with AJ holding the ball in his right hand and me dragging him in by his left hand. I know it sounds mean, but it was just as hard for me to follow through with teaching this particular lesson as it was for AJ to learn it.

We called for the manager, who asked us what we needed. Through tears, AJ held out the ball and haltingly blurted out the words, "God has convicted me of stealing. Would you please forgive me?"

This scene of a little boy being so sincere was so touching that the lady manager started crying also, and she said, "It's okay!"

"No, it's not okay!" I exclaimed. "It's stealing! So don't tell him it's okay when he is asking you to forgive him!"

"I forgive you!" cried the manager, taking the ball back.

As we drove home, I asked AJ, "Well, do you think you ever want to steal anything from a store again?"

"No, Dad! Never again!" he replied through deep, calming breaths. He learned a valuable lesson that day: there are consequences for dishonest behavior.

But the story doesn't end there. Ten years later, when I picked up AJ from high school one day and asked him how his day was, he told me something very interesting:

"In parenting class today, the teacher asked a question that no one had an answer for, except me."

My curiosity was piqued. "What was the question?" I asked.

"The question was, 'What would you do if your child ever stole something from a store?' So I raised my hand and gave the answer," said AJ.

And that, my friends, is a life lesson not quickly forgotten.

CHAPTER 6

When Should I Have "That Talk" with My Children?

*I do not want you to be **uninformed**.*
1 Corinthians 12:1 ESV

When is the right time to tell your children about how they were brought into this world? Please don't tell them that "the stork brought them" or that they were left on the doorstep in a basket. Slavic parents like to tell their kids that they found them in the cabbage patch in their garden! But kids won't believe these things for very long.

The time is right when you notice that your child begins to show an interest. They might mention something that tells you they already have some information about this, and now they are curious to learn more. That is what happened with AJ. He was about nine years old at the time. One day he walked into the kitchen and casually said, "Hey, Dad! Know what I learned in school today?"

Hesitant, I replied, "What, Son?"

"My teacher told us in health class that I have forty-six chromosomes, twenty-three from you and twenty-three from Mom!"

"Yes, that's right, Son," I responded, nervous about what might come next.

"Well, Dad, I was thinking—how did your twenty-three chromosomes get into Mommy's tummy?"

"Good question!" I blurted out. "I will get back to you on that."

To my relief, he contentedly wandered off to play with his toys. I remember thinking, *These kids today are too smart! It looks like it's time to have that conversation and answer his question.*

It surprised me that AJ already had more information on the subject than I thought he had. I felt like the dad who noticed too late that his son had already entered into puberty. As the story goes, that father finally prepared himself to bring up with his son the delicate subject of where babies come from. He nervously cleared his throat a few times, and then he carefully began his approach to his fourteen-year-old son: "Uh, Son—it's about time we had that discussion about, you know, um, sex."

"Sure, Dad!" responded the boy cheerfully. "What do you wanna know?"

Oops! Don't wait that long to talk with your son, as

it will then be too late. Instead, I asked God for the right timing to continue this conversation with my son.

About six months later, I was taking my two sons to a hockey game for a boys' night out. We were driving to the arena when I heard the still, small voice of God prompt me: "Now is the time!"

I gathered up my courage and started the conversation: "Hey, AJ! Do you remember your question about how my twenty-three chromosomes got into Mommy's tummy?"

"Yeah, Dad! So how did they?" he asked.

I told him about how boys and girls have different body parts, and how when they grow up and fall in love and get married, those parts fit together perfectly. I used the proper scientific names and explained the procedure, careful to emphasize that they are not embarrassed while doing this because they love each other so much.

Because I was driving, I had to keep my eyes on the road, but out of the corner of my eye I could see AJ grimacing and making disgusted-looking faces as I explained. But his younger brother, Luke, was looking straight ahead and grinning. His expression said, "No big deal."

"So, guys," I ventured bravely, "do you have any questions?"

There was a moment of dead silence. Then AJ finally asked, "Do I have to do that when I am married?"

"No," I said. "But then you probably wouldn't get married."

"Oh no, Dad! I want to get married!" he exclaimed. "But do I **have** to do that if I'm married?" he asked anxiously.

"Son," I replied, "you don't have to; you want to!"

That was AJ and Luke's introduction to the "facts of life." We drove on to the hockey game and ended up having a great evening.

Honestly, it was a bit scary to share so openly with the boys, but afterward, I was so happy that they learned about this from their father rather than in an ungodly way. Two kids down, one more to go—my daughter, Larissa.

A few years later, when my daughter was approaching her teen years, she began to ask questions that told us it was the right time to have "that talk" with her.

"Now it's your turn," I said to my wife, Esty. "I talked to the boys; now you talk to our daughter." Fathers are the best people to speak to their young boys, while moms are more effective having that chat with their daughters. You never want to embarrass your children or make them feel uncomfortable by your discussion.

Esty was smarter than I was. She went and bought a book from the Christian bookstore that was written specifically for daughters, and she and Larissa went into our bedroom and read it together. After about ten minutes, Larissa burst out of our bedroom, marched into her room, and slammed the door. Esty peeked out of our bedroom, laughing silently.

"What happened?" I mouthed to her.

"Tell you later!" was her response. Later that day, I found out what happened. When Esty and Larissa reached the part of the book that fully explained the process of making a baby, Larissa looked at my wife in stunned silence.

Then Larissa said to her in a sarcastic voice, **"And you call yourself a Christian?!!!"**

Larissa's vehement reaction so took Esty by surprise that she started to laugh.

Larissa had one more question: **"And you did it three times?"** (Larissa was our third and final child.) Then she stormed out of the bedroom. We still laugh when we remember that conversation!

Sexuality is such an important topic to discuss with your children. Many parents feel embarrassed to even approach this topic with any of their children—so they don't. The result is that the child learns about sexuality from other sources, whether from a schoolmate, from another child, or through pornographic images. This can be damaging because then the child is not learning about sexuality through the lens of God's intended purpose and beauty, within the limits of biblical morality, but is learning about it in a raw, unrestricted, "no rules" kind of way.

God created sex as a wonderful gift that permanently binds a man and a woman, and this is best expressed when a man and a woman join themselves together in love through marriage in the presence of God and witnesses—for life. It is a solemn vow and a covenant to a lifelong commitment that is protected by God's healthy boundaries.

As parents, we are the ones best suited to explain this to our children, and we can do so in a God-honoring way. This conversation should not be left to their friends or to some stranger at school. This is the time to be brave, dear parent!

CHAPTER 7:

Vision, Direction, and Identity

Your eyes saw my unformed substance; in your book were
written, every one of them, the days that were formed for
me, when as yet there was none of them.
Psalm 139:16 ESV

"Seeing" the Vision of Your Child

This is a topic that can easily be misunderstood. Psalm 139:16 speaks of **what God sees** while we are still in our mother's womb. David, the author of the psalm, refers to a "book" that has our "days" written in it.

Let me first state what I **don't** believe this passage is saying.

It does **not** say that we have **no choices**. It does **not** say that everything that happens to us is what God wrote down beforehand, and that is why our lives are the way they are. No—that is fatalism, and it prevents us from exercising our free will and making choices as humans.

I believe this verse speaks to what God calls us to do and what He calls our children to achieve. The chapters or pages of our "life book" He is referring to speak of what He has planned for us to accomplish in our lifetimes. Put another way, I think He has outlined the chapter headings of our life book, and our obedience to His will fills in the pages of our lives.

God has choices, and we have choices. He chooses our DNA, our height, our parents, where we are born, and our skin, eye, and hair colors. He is also the One who chooses our talents and abilities from birth. All of these choices that He has made enable and equip us to accomplish the purpose for which He created us. When we finally realize what that purpose is, it is then that we experience the deepest satisfaction of our lives. We discover that we actually love to do what we were designed and equipped by God to do.

So what are the things that **we** choose? We choose to either follow His purpose in our lives or to live according to our own selfish passions and desires. Our choices do matter. We can daily observe people who have made wise choices, and also those who have made poor choices, based on the good and bad outcomes they experience as a result of their decisions.

To the extent of our responsibility as fathers, how

can we help our children realize God's purpose for their lives? Do we tell them what vocation to follow? Is it our place to choose their life's work? I emphatically say "No!" in response to those questions.

I believe that the correct approach is to help our children discern what God's purpose for them is. That is, we as parents can desire to have eyes that perceive the vision God has for our children. After all, God is the One who has already given them the tools they need to reach that goal in the first place.

To help you better understand what I am saying, I can share with you what occurred in my own childhood and in that of my children.

The Vision God Gave My Dad Concerning Me

Growing up in an immigrant family, we faced the challenge of blending two different cultures and languages in our home. My parents spoke very little English because they came to this country from Ukraine as refugees through war-torn Germany only four years before my birth in New Jersey. As a result, we spoke Ukrainian at home.

My greatest desire as a small child was for my parents to learn to master the English language, and their desire for me was that I learn to speak, read, and write Ukrainian. To achieve their goal, they sent me to a Ukrainian school on Saturday mornings. This was definitely not to my liking! I distinctly remember the day when I was five or six years old and I asked my dad why he was forcing me to go to school on Saturdays and learn a language I would really have no use for in America.

His answer to me became the foundation of my life and ministry: "Son, you have to learn Ukrainian because one day God will open the borders to that country, and you will tell people there about Jesus in their native language!"

My dad told me this around 1959 at the height of the Cold War between the Soviet Union and the United States. In 1960, Nikita Khrushchev, then the leader of the powerful Soviet Union, banged his shoe on the table at a United Nations meeting in New York and openly declared to the West: "We will bury you!"

Only ten years after my dad's pronouncement of God's destiny for me, at the age of sixteen, I would record our first album in Ukrainian with my sister Rosita, her husband, John, and my best friend, Paul. Our songs soon became very popular on the shortwave radio broadcasts into the Soviet Union, which had banned the general public from all Christian activities.

Three years later, in 1973, we made our first journey to the Soviet Union, visiting the few registered churches that were allowed, visiting fifteen cities during a period of fifty days. It was then that I realized the value of my dad's vision of my future. Thanks to his foresight, I was able to sing and share my faith in Ukrainian on that historic trip.

Who would have thought that this early prophecy by my dad about me learning Ukrainian would come true? At that time, the Soviet Union was a mighty monolith composed of fifteen republics that spanned nine times zones and had more than 120 different languages. No one ever thought that in 1991 it would fragment into separate and independent nations without a war or without even a shot being fired. Who could have predicted that the Soviet Union would break up and public expressions of faith would be allowed in that land for the first time after seventy years of atheism?

But God knew, and He whispered it into my father's heart concerning his son George.

During the next fifty-year period, our singing group would record twenty-five more albums in three different languages. Since that first visit to the Soviet Union in 1973, I have visited Ukraine and the former republics of the USSR more than 110 times, preaching in Ukrainian to thousands of people in large stadiums in many cities and villages of Ukraine.

Let me make one thing very clear—my dad **did not** call me into the ministry, nor did he direct my future or my decisions. Rather, he heard from God and facilitated what I needed in preparation for what God would call me to do for Him.

This is what I want to emphasize for you fathers. If

you pray, if you ask God how best to facilitate for your children the future that God has for them, He will direct you. Just remember, you are **not** the ones to make their decisions for them. They must do that entirely on their own as they mature and seek God. It is more a matter of observing them, praying for them, and discerning what interests them. Psychologists call this "active listening."

I say this not only because it happened in my life, but because it is also what occurred with our children.

God's Direction for My Children

Esty and I got married in 1981 and were soon ready to start our family. One Sunday afternoon I returned to my church office and spent time on my knees asking God about the future of the children He would give us.

I distinctly remember promising God that if He gave me a son, that firstborn would be dedicated back to Him. God could call him to be a pastor, a missionary, or a minister of any kind. God's answer to that totally surprised me. He spoke to me: "He will not be a minister; he will be a doctor."

At first, I thought I misheard that quiet voice of God speaking to my thoughts. So, I repeated my promise to God: He could call my son to be a pastor, a missionary, or a minister—whatever God wanted. The firstborn belongs to God, as the Bible teaches.

Again, God spoke the same words: "He will not be a minister; he will be a doctor."

As I pondered this second confirmation of God's voice, I remember thinking, *Okay, then; at least he won't be poor!*

Sure enough, at eight years of age, my firstborn son, AJ, told us that he wanted to be a doctor when he grew up. Today, he is a successful surgeon practicing in Orlando, Florida, where he lives with his wife, Whitney, and their two children, Adelaide and Graham.

Things happened differently with my second-born child, Luke. He was in high school and was not certain what career direction he should take. My wife suggested that he take a psychology course and see if he liked that. Over a period of time, and after exploring this career option in college, Luke dedicated himself to pursue a vocation related to the field of psychology. God has equipped him with an empathetic and tender heart that drew him to become a "healer," with a focus on mental health.

Being a pastor and being somewhat familiar with counseling people, I asked Luke if he was ready to hear difficult stories of abuse and neglect from hurting people. I will never forget his reply: "Dad, Jesus did not come to heal the healthy people. He came to heal the sick ones."

I understood. God had put this desire in his heart. My response to him was, "Luke, if you are willing to do that, then God is truly calling you to that ministry."

Today, Luke is a successful psychologist. He is an officer in the US Air Force, treating the men and women of our military who return from war with post-traumatic stress disorder (PTSD), as well as helping our military members in the areas of suicide prevention and alcohol, drug, and sexual abuse. Luke is currently stationed in Georgia with his wife, Whitney (yes, we have two Whitneys!), and their three children—Harper, Stella, and Tatum.

I again want to emphasize that actively listening to your children can help you release them to the vocations that **they** are drawn to, not to what **you** decide for them. Parents who try to dictate and micromanage their children's career choices often end up creating resentment from their grown children who were not allowed to pursue their passions.

We named our third and final child, a daughter, Larissa Joy. Our family was complete. As we watched our daughter grow up, we noticed that she had teaching ability, so we encouraged her to follow that path. She graduated college with a teaching degree and had great success teaching at a charter school near Charlotte, North Carolina, where we previously lived.

Today we live near Larissa and her husband, Isaac, in Springfield, Missouri, where she has dedicated herself to fulfilling the role of a mother to their three children—Canon, Aspen, and Mila.

That brings the number of our grandchildren to eight. Our role now is to pray for and encourage each of the children of our children!

Fathers Contribute to the Identity of Their Children

How can fathers help to develop the identity of their children?

Both parents must fulfill their God-given roles. By nature, moms often pay more attention to details within the home to make their "nest" comfortable for their family. They love to nurture the little ones, feed them, and wash and clothe them so that they are healthy and well fed. Men, by nature, often tend to be more "hunters" and "gatherers" who work hard outside the home to provide needed resources to meet the family's needs.

The best kind of home, though, is one where the father *participates* in helping to raise his children.

A father can dramatically increase the success of his children's future by taking up his share of the child-raising responsibilities in his home. Unfortunately, in our society today, there are far too many homes where the father is missing. Divorce has severely fractured the once-solid foundation of our families. Single mothers have to raise their children without a father, and this leads to greater challenges regarding the growth and social development of the children.

Young boys who grow up without the steadying influence of a male role model will often seek approval from other boys and will become more influenced by their peers. Young girls who do not have a loving father to demonstrate the appropriate male image can become romantically involved with boys much earlier than they would otherwise because they seek the protection and love that only a father can provide.

If a father is too busy working to spend any time with his children, or if he is just following his own pursuits or hobbies, he has completely neglected his role as a father.

Fathers, your children don't want more "things;" they want **you**.

Not only does this obligate us to spend more time with our families, but it also requires us to be careful with our words and actions, both with our spouse and with our children.

Careless or angry words can damage and lower the self-esteem of our children, and sadly, there are fathers who have severely damaged those living in their homes. Under the influence of alcohol or drugs, careless fathers speak hurtful words that wound the spirit of a child, or they explode into uncontrollable rage that results in physical or emotional abuse of the wife and children. For those unhappy children, home is not a place of love and comfort, to say the least.

Fathers Influence Our God Concepts

The role of a father is so important in the family because he is the child's first male authority figure. The way that children learn to respond to their fathers tends to be the way they relate to other people, to authority figures, and to God. Please understand that I don't think this is absolute in all cases, but a child's relationship with their father does influence that child positively or negatively to some degree.

If a father is distant, unaffectionate, or unapproachable, God may appear distant to the young child later in life.

If a father is harsh, overly strict, and only rules-based, God may seem to be difficult to please.

If a father is absent or uncaring, then God, too, may seem indifferent to the child. The child may think, *God is up there somewhere, but He must not care about me or want to be involved in my life.*

If the father is angry and abusive, yet religious at the same time, the child will not want to have anything to do with God because of this hypocrisy. Who wants to serve a God who is angry with them all the time?

All of these distorted God-concepts are false. God is actually not distant, but He is very near to anyone who desperately needs Him and who will call upon Him for help.

God is never harsh or only rules-based. Yes, He is

holy and asks us to follow His example, but at the same time, He gives us the grace or divine assistance to obey Him willingly, along with the power to live the Christian life. That is the "grace" that He provides for us.

God is definitely not indifferent to our hurts and needs. He is as near as our prayer to Him. Wherever you are, or whatever trouble you are in—sincerely and honestly call out to Him, and He will answer the cry of your heart.

Lastly, God is not angry with us because we have fallen or have disobeyed His holy standards. In fact, Our heavenly Father grieves for us when He sees the pain and suffering that our wrong choices bring upon us. His great love for us is why He sent His Son, Jesus, to save and deliver us from our sin.

John 3:16 is quoted so often that we miss the power of these words: "For God so loved the world, that he gave his only Son" (ESV).

Friends, God loves us. He loves us just the way we are—broken, hurting, willful, careless—the list goes on. Our Father in heaven loves His children, and His heart aches to hug and embrace us, just as the father of the lost son did.

In every reference to his heavenly Father, Jesus speaks of the Father's great love, compassion, and patience with sinful man. In fact, Jesus came to show us what God the Father is really like. He is just like Jesus—or more accurately, Jesus is like Him. That is also what God wants us as men and as fathers to be like. He wants us to be loving and kind to our children and to our families.

I encourage you men to become the kind of fathers who raise healthy, God-loving children; or in the case of a son who was hurt by an abusive father, I encourage you to become a better father to your children than your father was to you.

Dads, you have a great deal to do with the vision, direction, and identity of your children. Your parenting helps to mold the soft clay of their hearts and minds.

CHAPTER 8:

Childhood Training

Train up a child in the way he should go,
and when he is old he will not depart from it.
Proverbs 22:6 NKJV

This chapter is for both parents. After all, both mothers and fathers could use a few bits of advice about raising well-adjusted children! Dad, I included this chapter in this book to help you understand how you, as a father, can reinforce the lessons your wife has begun in your children's lives. I did this with my children when my wife, Esty, worked an occasional evening shift as a hospital nurse.

Teach Them to Respect Your Routines

A **routine** brings stability, security, and comfort to a child and reinforces good behavior and discipline in a child's life. A routine helps them to understand what you expect from them, and they learn to behave accordingly. If you are inconsistent as a parent, don't expect your children to be consistent; disorganization and chaos are sure to follow.

When our children know what to expect at mealtimes, when they know when they should be doing their homework, and when they know the routine for getting ready for school or church, they adjust to these activities. This is especially true at bedtimes.

In my travels as an evangelist, I have stayed in many homes and have observed parents who let their children stay up late on school nights, doing homework at a very late hour. There was **no consistency** for these children, and as a result, when the parents called for the children to go to bed, there was much resistance from them.

"Can't we stay up a little longer?" "You said okay last time." "We don't want to go to bed now. Do we have to?"

Each night would be a new battle of wills. Let me ask you—who is the authority here? Is it you, or is it your child?

I saw this dynamic illustrated when I read about a visiting Chinese pastor who was once imprisoned for his faith by the Communist government during Chairman Mao's regime. When released from prison and then expelled from his native country, he came to America and shared his story in churches across our nation, from New York to California. He also stayed in many peoples' homes during his tour of America.

When asked by the press what caught his attention the most during his travels across this land of freedom compared to his home country of China, his reply surprised the reporters: "I was amazed how well the parents obeyed the children in your country."

What an indictment of the laxness and inconsistency of American parents! Even though this Chinese pastor came from an oppressive and atheistic regime, the children in that country still showed their parents and grandparents great respect and held them in high regard. These values are missing now in our country.

Keep a Schedule with Your Kids

Allow me to share what I discovered to be most effective in keeping a consistent schedule with my children. I speak as a father who had two energetic boys and a quieter, more compliant daughter.

If it was a day when Esty worked the 3 to 11 p.m. shift at the hospital, I would come home earlier from my job as pastor of our church, either at three or four o'clock. Our home schedule went something like this: The kids came home from school and had a small snack, and then we got the homework out of the way first. As soon as the homework was done, I took the kids to the park if the weather was nice, and I played outside with them until supper.

It is important to eat together as a family at supper-time whenever possible. When Esty had to work at the hospital, we reheated what she had prepared earlier in the day, and after supper the kids could play indoors until bath time.

We never had issues with schedules because I found a creative way to implement them. Bath time was at 8:00 p.m. on the dot. At 7:30, I would go into the room where they were playing and tell them, "Okay, kids, bath time in thirty minutes, so you can still play for half an hour."

"Okay, Dad!" They thought I had given them an additional half hour! Fifteen minutes later, I would go in again and make another announcement: "You have fifteen more minutes, kids! You can keep playing."

The reply would be, "Thanks, Dad!" as if I had given them even more time.

When it was 7:55, I paid them one more visit, telling them they had five minutes more.

The result? At 8:00 p.m., they knew it was time, and they never asked for more time because I had given them three opportunities to play "longer."

Read Books to Your Children

After bath time, I would read books to them before bed. This takes time, but it stimulates their appetite for learning. Get good Christian books that teach character, books that tell stories about the heroes of the Bible, or even nature books about the amazing world God has created.

The rule was that the children had to be in bed on a school night by 8:30 p.m., or 8:45 p.m. at the latest. They couldn't get out of bed after that, but they could read books as much as they wanted before going to sleep. I installed a night lamp over their beds so they could continue reading books after I left the room. I was not worried about them staying up too late. I would rather have them fall asleep while reading or looking at the pictures in the nature books than watching television or, in today's world, glued to their devices.

This practice cultivated in each of my three children a love of reading that served them well as they pursued college and graduate schools later in life.

Pray with Your Children

After we had read together, I would kneel down by their bedside, and in their very young years, they would repeat short prayers after me. When they were able to pray out loud on their own, I had them do so. I could tell you many stories of the wonderful things that they prayed by themselves.

Following the breakup of the Soviet Union, there

were incredible opportunities to travel to Ukraine and share the gospel in large stadiums and concert halls. As a result, I began to travel there for a week at a time.

My firstborn was only seven when I began to conduct those early evangelistic crusades, and I remember telling him that Daddy had to leave home for a week or so. AJ didn't understand the concept of a week yet, so he asked, "Daddy, how many sleeps is that?"

I took his fingers and counted out ten fingers. "That's too long Daddy!" he protested.

"It's okay, Son. Daddy has to go there and tell people about Jesus. I will come back soon and bring you a present when I come home," I answered, hoping to mollify him.

That night, we knelt by the bed and prayed. It was AJ's turn to pray. He said, "Jesus, I don't want my daddy to go to Ukraine."

Wow. That was pretty honest for a little boy. I wonder what he will pray next? I thought.

After a moment, AJ continued: "But Jesus, I know my dad has to go to tell people about You, so please bless him there and bring him back safely home."

I couldn't speak. A knot formed in my throat. A little boy who loves his dad fiercely enough to complain to God, but then surrenders him back. That is powerful. I never forgot that prayer, and I observed how even little children can honor the highest authority in our home. What a lesson!

This is one of the reasons you shouldn't allow your children to pray "silently." You will miss out on hearing similar touching prayers from your children. Another reason could be that they might not be praying at all, but are just coasting on your prayers instead. Like anything else in childhood, prayer is a discipline that must be learned and practiced.

There are many different ways to pray together as a family. Some like to pray as a concert of prayer where everyone prays at the same time. With my children, I liked to have them pray one at a time, listening to each other's prayers. This helped me to "hold a pulse" on their spiritual condition. Praying out loud in front of their siblings also taught them courage and discipline. Once we started praying like that, it became a natural habit, and the kids did it without complaining or protesting. **Kids will do what you teach them to do, and they will do so consistently**. It is not rocket science.

Limit "Screen Time"

The explosion of the use of smart phones and tablets has come to dominate our free time in a very invasive way. Adults and children alike are glued to their screens, and all conversation stops while we scroll for "likes" and flick through staged portraits of our friends.

These habits are not healthy for children or for their

development. According to Dr. Liraz Margalit:

> In order for the brain's neural networks to develop normally during the critical period, a child needs specific stimuli from the **outside** environment . . . These essential stimuli are not found on today's tablet screens. When a young child spends too much time in front of a screen and not getting enough required stimuli from the real world, their development becomes stunted.[2]

Granted, giving your child a tablet is an easy "babysitter," but please limit that time each day if you want your child to develop healthy habits in life. That also means setting an example for them by limiting your own screen time when spending time with them, especially at mealtimes. Phones off, people!

Teach Your Children the "Gift of Chores"

How can we develop a good work ethic in our children? No one wants lazy kids. What is the answer? Give your children small jobs or tasks that they can do, like vacuuming the floor, washing dishes, or helping to clean the garage or their rooms.

My wife, Esty, recalls growing up on a farm where she had to feed chickens early in the morning before school.

She also had to milk cows and, in the summer, help her dad work in the fields. She developed a very strong work ethic that greatly benefitted our family. As a result, our children learned motivation and self-discipline from her at a very young age that helped them achieve very difficult goals in their academics and sports.

Is it easy to get your child to do work? No—it is a struggle in any family. Yet if you make the hard choices and pursue this diligently now, viewing a good work ethic as a value that will greatly benefit your children's efforts in school and in their future careers, it will make it easier for them later in life:

> Even though it is more difficult at the time to persist in having children do chores, kids benefit from the experience. Research indicates that those children who do have a set of chores have higher self-esteem, are more responsible, and are better able to deal with frustration and delay gratification, all of which contribute to greater success in school.[3]

"Oh, they are too young still," you say. "They have time to learn that." You might be surprised, then, at this bit of research by Rossman: "The best predictor of young adults' success in their mid-20's was that they participated in household tasks when they were three or four."[4]

It will always be a challenge, but let's raise up a generation of children with discipline, perseverance, and hard work so they can successfully face the increasingly tough challenges of the society in which we live. Work is honorable; laziness is not. Start when they are little.

CHAPTER 9:

How Do I Protect My Family? Part 1

Prayer

There was a man in the land of Uz whose name was Job, and that man was blameless and upright, one who feared God and turned away from evil. There were born to him seven sons and three daughters . . . He would rise early in the morning and offer burnt offerings according to the number of them all.

Job 1:1–2, 5 ESV

"How do I protect my family?" That really is a great question. I am sure that you will agree that most parents are not just concerned about the physical safety of their children, but they are also concerned about their children's spiritual and emotional protection. The least I can do is convey to you, dear readers, what my wife,

Esty, and I did. It might not be the complete answer for everyone, but it certainly worked for our three children.

My response can be summed up with the following three points, each of which requires action on our part as fathers:

1. Pray fervently and daily for your children and with them.
2. Limit their freedom wisely, with clear explanations.
3. Communicate clearly and often with them, sharing life experiences.

Each of these three actions will be explained and illustrated with simple and easy-to-understand examples. In this chapter, we will discuss the first action word: prayer. Chapter 10 will continue with the next two action words: limit and communicate.

We begin with prayer. There are a lot of men in the Bible who prayed, but let me tell you about a father who prayed powerfully and effectively for his family. This man had a large family—ten children! By any standard, that is a lot of mouths to feed. You would think that with so many kids, he couldn't pay attention to them all, or that he might lose track of where a few of them were in their lives. But not this father.

He prayed for each of them every day. In fact, his prayers were so effective that the devil complained to God that he could not touch this man's family! This man was named Job. Much has been said about the suffering of Job, but for the moment, let's look at Job's faithfulness as a father.

In the first chapter of the book of Job, we discover that Job's children were much like our own today. They loved celebrations at each other's homes, they visited each other, and they enjoyed the good food and fun activities that siblings in a healthy relationship love doing together. But their father, Job, still prayed for them. Like a lot of fathers, he worried about his children.

Maybe, he thought, *just maybe, they might have done or said something that dishonors God in some way.*

So Job did what fathers in that patriarchal time did—he offered burnt sacrifices to God on behalf of his children. Although the Bible does not specifically say that he prayed, common sense dictates that he must have prayed as he offered those sacrifices, as a prayer of dedication accompanied every sacrifice to God. The Bible also tells us that Job consecrated his children. That means he gave them to God. This is powerful! Our children were born to us, but they really belong to God, and Job understood this well.

Today we are no longer required to offer sacrifices to God by bringing burnt offerings like Job did. Jesus, the Son of God, became the supreme sacrifice for us, once and for all time. But as fathers, we still can pray. In fact, it should not just be that we *can* pray, but that we *must* pray!

The passage goes on to say that Job did this continually. What a faithful father! He never stopped praying! It is no wonder that the devil himself complained about this protection to God. Listen to the devil's whining: "Have you not put a hedge around him and his house and all that he has, on every side?" (Job 1:10 ESV).

What does he mean by the word "hedge"? Back in Job's day, farmers used to grow large bushes around their territory to protect the fields where their animals grazed. The bushes grew very thick with long, needle-sharp thorns that prevented wild animals from entering the fields and attacking their sheep or livestock. What a descriptive analogy as to what effective prayer can do!

Praying a "hedge of thorns" around your home is also extremely effective for us today. The verse mentions spiritual protection in three areas: "a hedge **around him** and **his house** and **all that he has** on every side?" (Job 1:10 ESV).

Just think about that, fathers. God put a hedge of protection around Job, his house, and all that he had—on every side—all because Job rose early in the morning to bring a sacrifice to God on behalf of his children. Wouldn't you want that kind of protection around your home and family?

Someone might ask, "But didn't God allow all Job's children to perish in one day? What kind of protection is that?" Yes, that terrible tragedy did happen, but not because of anything that Job or his children did wrong.

God allowed an innocent man to suffer horribly in order to prove to Satan that Job would still love and serve Him even if everything Job loved was taken away from him.

Job's later testing was a rare and unusual situation that God carefully controlled for a specific purpose. The truth of the matter is that this father's prayers of protection were so effective that even the devil himself could not penetrate them!

At the end of the book of Job, we read that God gave Job a double portion of everything that had been taken away from him. He had twice as many animals, and God gave him ten more beautiful children.

"Wait!" you say. "That's not twice as many children. God took away ten children and only gave back ten more. How is that double?"

We are forgetting that God sees eternity much differently than we do. We see our limited time here on the earth as the most important time of our existence. Yet when you compare a ninety-year life span with countless trillions of centuries in eternity, our life here is less than a blink of an eye. Job's children who died were waiting for him in heaven, and now he has twenty children total—exactly double.

In the New Testament, we see that Jesus Himself often withdrew to the wilderness or climbed up a mountain to pray at night. It was in these places where He received strength to preach and teach and heal the broken people who came to Him each day. The Son of God, in speaking of His Father's house, quoted the prophet Isaiah: "Is it not written: 'My house shall be a house of prayer for all nations'?" (Mark 11:17 ESV).

Growing up in my father's house, I experienced first-hand the benefits of my father's prayers for me. When I was a child, my father prayed with me each morning by our front door before I went to school. Many times I would come home from school, open the door to my father's office, and see him kneeling by a chair, praying fervently for our family. I would softly close the door again, inwardly pleased and thankful that my father was such a man of prayer. What a sense of peace and security it brought me! Dad is praying for me!

Those prayers protected me spiritually in ways that I cannot even imagine or understand, especially during my teenage years. I am where I am in ministry today because of the prayers and faithfulness of my father interceding for me on his knees. In fact, these memories of my father praying for me are one of the reasons why I named this book *In My Father's House*.

Prayer is such a simple act, yet in our busy, technologically connected world where we can't be a day without our smartphones, we neglect to set aside time to withdraw from the distractions of our texts and notifications—and simply pray.

When I became a father for the first time, I felt anxious and unsure of myself. Could I ever become the faithful man of prayer for my children that my father was for me? At the age of twenty-nine, this really worried me! Would my children love and serve the Lord as my siblings and I did?

God answered my question in a way that calmed my heart. I'll never forget what He whispered to my heart one day: "You do your part as a father and pray with your children, and I will do My part and bless them!" How grateful I was to hear these reassuring words from God!

From the time that my three children could speak their first words, we taught them to pray. At first we had them repeat the prayers after us, word by word, and later, when they were able, they prayed their own prayers. We would do this each night after one of us read them a bedtime story, and this became a normal part of our lives.

When my children were old enough to go to school, I practiced what my father did with me—we prayed at the front door. I added a particular prayer at the end—a prayer of putting on the **armor of God.**

In **Ephesians 6,** Paul encourages all Christians to prepare for spiritual warfare. He mentions six articles of armor for protection. I prayed with my children for these different pieces of armor to be placed on us. Together, we would make the motions with our hands that we were "putting on" these pieces of armor for spiritual protection for the day. Our prayers sounded something like this:

> We put on our heads the **helmet of salvation**, and on our hearts the **breastplate of righteousness**. On our waist we put on the **belt of truth**, and on our feet the **sandals of peace**. We lift up the **shield of faith** to quench the fiery darts of the wicked one, and we hold in our hand the **sword of the Spirit**!

Perhaps this might sound too literal for some, but we did this faithfully every single morning from kindergarten through high school for all three children. Every morning we would pause at the front door and faithfully pray this prayer.

When my boys were both in high school, they often liked to wake up at the last minute and rush off to school, but we still prayed this prayer at the door, even though the words came out in a hurry.

"Dad, we are going to be late!"

"Too bad. Next time get up earlier. Now pray."

Think what you want, but the result was that God kept my children faithful to Him through all their school years. I know it was prayer that helped and protected them in this regard.

My three children are now all grown and married, living in their own homes with children of their own. Believe it or not, Esty and I still pray every day for them by name, as well as for their spouses and our eight grandchildren. Even though it's just the two of us now,

Esty and I also still put on the armor of God and pray a hedge of thorns around our loved ones each day. Why? Because it is such a powerful prayer! Try it and see.

CHAPTER 10:

How Do I Protect My Family? Part 2

Limitations and Communication

How can a young man keep his way pure?
By guarding it according to Your word.
Psalm 119:9 ESV

We are in a spiritual battle. Whether you sense it or not, unseen demonic forces are increasingly wreaking havoc in our world. Our children face much greater temptations than we faced in our childhood.

There are those who were not born in the United States who say that the morality in their country of birth was better than it is here. Yet they are not aware that forty years ago, America also had a very conservative culture. Sadly, we see family values eroding today, not just in this country, but all over the world. If you return to your country of birth, you will likely discover that the place where you grew up is not as safe as it used to be. There is an explosion of immorality, idolatry, and violence that threatens to destabilize the very foundations of society.

The family structure is being destroyed in the name of tolerance. Traditional marriages are breaking apart. So many mothers are raising their children alone. Where are the fathers? In many cases, they are abandoning their wives and children to pursue the freedom to do only what they want. Broken marriages, divorces, and selfishness have greatly damaged families today.

"Our parents were too strict!" some men complain. "Let the kids have some freedom." But it is easy to forget that true freedom is accompanied by wise limitations. Someone wisely said, "Freedom is not the right to do whatever we want; true freedom is the power to do what is right."

Just as a red traffic light restricts freedom of movement, only to give more freedom for traffic to flow smoothly when the light is green shortly thereafter, so God's Word gives us wise limitations so that we don't destroy our lives and the lives of others. Society functions better when people obey the law. It falls apart when everyone decides to do whatever he or she wants to do.

A wise father is one who is assumes his responsibility as a leader in his home. He knows where his children are and what they are doing. He is aware of who their friends are. He makes wise rules in the home to protect his children and his family. Let's discuss some limits we need to place on our children.

Because today's technology has placed real-time communication into personal devices, accessibility to evil has also increased. Our children can easily download—right to their cell phone or tablet—television shows that casually promote immorality, movies that glorify rebellion and gratuitous killing, and computer games that illustrate demonic violence and bloodshed. Teenagers, who already experience turbulent hormones, can watch hardcore pornography on their smart phones or tablets without their parents even knowing about it.

Texting and real-time video communication make it possible for children to send each other sexually explicit pictures or videos of themselves—even if they are not in the same room together! This has been dubbed "sexting," or texting with sexual images. Too many parents do not even have a clue as to what their children are doing or what they are capable of doing. Even worse, anyone who has that teenager's email or mobile number can text or email them explicit images, even if the child has not actively sought those images out.

Perverted, middle-aged child predators are lurking online in chat rooms and teen sites, ready to prey upon naïve teenagers, pretending to be their age and luring them in with promised money to take their clothes off or engage in sexual acts on camera. They will attempt to get the child to compromise in some way, obtain pictures of them, and then threaten to expose them on the internet if they don't fulfill their evil fantasies even further. The child is then caught in a web of shame and fear of public exposure. Some have committed suicide because they were cornered into these horrible situations.

How can parents protect their children? Let me share three practical suggestions to help limit your children's exposure to temptation on their electronic devices.

First, learn how to use the "restrictions" feature on their smart phones, tablets, or other devices. Those restrictions can limit the sites on the internet that the child can visit. There is a password you can put into place that they cannot change.

Secondly, check their phone randomly, at any time and without warning. Don't allow them to put a password on their phone that locks you out of their device.

Thirdly, place a restrictive application like Net Nanny, or similar blocking software, on all of your computers and tablets to avoid X-rated sites. Good programs will block any search requests or attempts to access restricted content on your computer. This is highly recommended!

For more ways to limit your child's online exposure to pornography, simply type the following query into your computer browser's search engine (such as Google or Bing): "How do I limit my child's exposure to pornography?" Then check out the links that will further guide you in making your child's device a safer experience for them.

These are just some outward, physical restrictions you can place on your child. These restrictions alone will not be enough to protect your child from harm. If a determined teenager wants to bypass your rules, they will find a way to hack those restrictions and get around them.

You have to reach your child's heart. Sit down with your child and effectively communicate the necessary boundaries that need to be put into place—not just by you, but also by your child. Talk to your child like an adult.

My father did this with me. When I entered the hormonal years of puberty, my dad told me a very personal story about how he kept his sexual purity during his single years. My dad is in heaven now, so I think I can safely tell this story. I must give a word of warning, though—it is pretty spicy! However, it made a very powerful impact on my life, especially during my own teenage years.

Before my dad married my mom, he worked in a factory with other men who were not followers of Jesus. One day, their conversation turned to the subject of women. When the men discovered that my dad was a virgin, they were shocked! Thinking that they were going to do him a favor, they hired a prostitute to wait for him in his bed on the evening of his birthday.

You can imagine my surprise to hear this scandalous story from my dad! It shocked me that my father, a spiritual giant in my eyes and the very dignified and respected pastor of our church, was telling me such an intimate and personally revealing story. Needless to say, he had my full teenage attention at this point.

My dad told me that he went into his dark apartment so exhausted from his day of work that he didn't even turn the lights on. He knelt by the side of his bed and said his prayers. Taking off his outer clothing, he slipped into his bed under the warm covers. It was then that he discovered there was a naked woman sharing his bed!

I remember thinking to myself, *This is incredible! A naked woman!* Remember, I was fourteen years old at the time!

"What did you do, Dad?" I asked him breathlessly.

"I switched the lights on," he said, "and there she was! Naked as the day she was born!"

"So, then what?"

"She began to reach for me, and I backed away, telling her to get out of my room!"

"Why?" she asked. "I'm paid for, so I'm yours for the night!"

My dad refused, and he made her leave his room. I was stunned by this very intimate, yet honest, account of my dad's encounter with temptation in his single years. More so than any sermon, it spoke to me of his determination to honor God and keep himself pure for his future wife one day.

I was fourteen years old when I heard that story, and that very day I made a promise to God and to myself that I, too, would keep myself pure for the one woman who would one day become my wife. This commitment kept me safe through my single years, and it continues to do so to this day as a married man.

Perhaps you don't have a similarly dramatic story to tell your sons as my dad did, but you can still sit down with your children when the time is right and share your heart. A father is a very powerful and effective communicator because of his position as the head of the home, especially when he summons the courage to overcome his personal shyness and speak to his teenagers about temptations that all young people face.

When my two sons reached their teen years, I shared this personal story about Dido (grandfather) with them. They, too, were pretty surprised that the patriarch of our family had been open enough to share that story with me. They had the same reaction that I had the first time I heard this story: "This happened to **our** Dido? No way! That's incredible!" It had the same positive impact on them as it did on me.

Your sons want to know that you understand the temptations they are facing. They want to hear from you that it's normal to go through what they are going through. Please remember that every teenager thinks that they are the only one to experience this strange rush of overwhelming hormones!

With my daughter, Larissa, I did something entirely different. When she turned thirteen, I went to a jewelry store and bought her a gold ring with a heart encircling a cross. I gave it to her and then explained what this ring symbolized:

> Larissa, this is what is called a promise ring. That means that you make me a promise to keep yourself pure until the day you marry. So for now, I am the man in your life. Always wear that ring. When you look at the ring, it will remind you that you belong to your dad. One day I will walk you down the aisle on your wedding day, and there will be another man waiting for you there at the front. Then you can give me this ring back because that man will give you another ring and will love you forever. You will then belong to him.

We both had tears in our eyes as she put that ring on. She was so touched by this gift that the next day she told all her friends at school that her dad gave her a promise ring and that she made a commitment to God and to me to stay pure until marriage. It was a powerful event in her life—so powerful that she never took that ring off until her wedding day years later.

On the day of her wedding, I walked Larissa down

the aisle in Branson, Missouri, in front of all our family and friends. My son Luke was conducting the marriage ceremony. Right before I gave her away to her future husband, Isaac, we stopped together at the front of the church. I had one more thing to tell her:

> Larissa, when you were thirteen years old, I gave you a promise ring and told you that I was your man. You promised to never take it off and to keep yourself pure until the day I walked you down the aisle to present you to another man who would be standing there, waiting for you. That day has finally come. Larissa, you can now give me that ring back, and I'll keep it for your children. I can safely give you away now because Isaac is waiting for you with another ring. Thank you for keeping your promise! Mom and I love you!

It was a very emotional moment for all of us. Every daughter wants her dad to make her feel special. Someone once said that the way a girl relates to her father will one day be the way she relates to her future husband, and I believe this to be true. If a father can maintain a truly close relationship with his daughter, he teaches her to respect and relate well to men.

On the other hand, when a daughter feels estranged or distant from her father, she may look for love in the arms of the first man who tells her the words she longs to hear—that's she's special, or beautiful. Those words can be powerful, yet can be misused by a man with selfish motives.

Fathers, make a special effort to be the man in your daughters' lives. Share openly with your sons about temptation. Give your children wise limitations about how to use their mobile devices and computers. You will be glad that you did.

CHAPTER 11:

Battling and Overcoming Addiction[5]

*Present your bodies a living and holy **sacrifice**, acceptable to God . . . And do not be conformed to this world, but be transformed by the **renewing of your mind**.*
Romans 12:1–2 NASB

Where do you think is the most difficult place for a man to be a spiritual example to others? Would it be in church? No—it is pretty easy to be a good Christian there. What about at work? That might be more of a challenge. I think you will agree with me when I say that the hardest place for a man to be a strong Christian is in his own home.

Home is often where our innermost thoughts and personal behaviors are the most relaxed and most un-guarded. Our families get to see the "real us" with all of our faults and habits. Outside our homes, we want to portray ourselves to others as strong leaders who always do the right thing.

At home, though, as my wife can tell you, all of my faults, mistakes, and character quirks can be clearly seen. The great thing is that my wife still loves me after almost forty years of living under the same roof!

One of the greatest responsibilities of being a good father and husband is to be the protector of his home. This is not just about physical protection and locking our front door, but it is also about spiritual protection over our home. Jesus described it this way: "But no one can enter a strong man's house and plunder his goods, unless he first ties up the strong man. Then indeed he may plunder his house" (Mark 3:27 ESV).

Fathers are the first line of defense against the enemy who seeks to attack their homes, wives, and children. If the devil can tie us up with any kind of sin, then he can get to our families more easily.

We all know that King David won many battles against countless enemies out on the battlefield. He also wrote numerous psalms that tell of his struggles against those who wanted to destroy him before he became king. David recognized where his toughest battle would take place: "I will walk **within my house** in the integrity of my heart" (Psalm 101:2 NASB). His toughest battle would take place in his home, in the beautiful palace where he lived as the most beloved king of Israel. This is where David would battle against a challenge he never faced before.

Although he was a brave warrior and was unafraid of the dangers of physical warfare, David recognized that his sensitive and romantic nature could lead him into a different kind of danger. With every good intention, David wrote these words in the following verse: "I will set nothing wicked before my eyes" (Psalm 101:3 NKJV).

Speaking of eyes, have you ever thought about why God called Job "a blameless and upright man, one who fears God and shuns evil" (Job 1:8 NKJV)? Could the reason be because Job made a promise to be careful of where he focused his attention? Notice his statements and commitments concerning his eyes:

> I made a covenant with my **eyes** not to look lustfully at a young woman. . . . For that would [be] wicked, a sin to be judged. It is a **fire** that burns to Destruction; it would have uprooted my harvest. (Job 31:1, 11–12 NIV)

Keep these verses about Job and his eyes in mind as we continue with the story of David.

All was well for David until the day that this mighty warrior grew weary of constant warfare, or perhaps just became bored, and stopped fighting God's battles. Instead of going out to the battlefield as usual, David decided to send out his generals in his place and just relax at home.

With too much time on his hands, King David spent the day on his couch. Later that evening, while strolling on the roof of his palace, he allowed his eyes to gaze upon the nakedness of a woman bathing on the roof next door.

You know the story. David's gaze turned into lust after another man's wife. That, in turn, led to him committing adultery with her. When the woman, Bathsheba, later told David that she was pregnant with his child, David found a way to deliberately murder her faithful husband on the battlefield while he was away at war. All this remained hidden until God revealed David's sin through the prophet Nathan. A sad chain of events followed that would affect David, his sons, and his kingdom.

David, invincible in battle, a young man who once defeated a mighty giant, allowed himself to be defeated by a tiny glance in the wrong direction. That's all it took. Disaster soon followed in the lives of his children.

To his great sorrow, that first baby born to Bathsheba died at birth. Later, one of David's sons, Amnon, raped his half-sister. Another son, Absalom, murdered that brother and later rebelled against his father. A third son, Adonijah, tried to declare himself king before his brother could. All this happened because the dad opened the door and let the Enemy attack his home and his family.

This same scourge of setting wickedness before our eyes that David described in Psalm 101 is severely affecting our society, especially men, today. Nothing else so consumes a man's thoughts as images of nudity and immorality. Is this so wrong? Is watching pornography sinful?

Yes! It violates the **purity** of your heart and spirit. Jesus said: "You have heard that it was said, 'You shall not commit adultery.' But I tell you that everyone who looks at a woman lustfully has already committed adultery with her **in his heart**" (Matthew 5:27–28 NIV). Jesus also said, "Everyone who practices sin is a **slave** to sin" (John 8:34 ESV). The Lord makes it clear that giving ourselves over to any sin results in slavery, or what we today call **addiction**. The Enemy seeks to bind and lead astray every head of the home, the father, in any way possible.

What is an addiction? An addiction is a compulsion, a very strong urge, to repeat an action or activity frequently, even if it is detrimental to us and to those we love.

There are many kinds of addictions, such as addictions to food, drugs, alcohol, or gambling. People can even be addicted to social media—checking your phone every five seconds!

Of all addictions, watching pornography has one of the strongest capabilities to become compulsive and habit forming. A behavior scientist writes:

Just like drugs and other addictive substances, porn floods the brain with chemicals, like dopamine. Over time, the brain gets overwhelmed by the constant overload of chemicals and starts to build up a **dependency** to pornography. Porn has the strongest tendency to be **addictive**! Porn creates deeper **compulsions** to watch **more** porn!

Porn has become the new drug of choice.

Solomon tells us, "There is nothing new under the sun" (Ecclesiastes 1:9 ESV). Sexual images were a problem even in Bible times! God reveals this to the prophet Ezekiel: "Then he said to me, 'Son of man, have you seen what the elders of the house of Israel are doing in the **dark**, each in his room of **pictures**? For they say, 'The Lord does not see us.'" (Ezekiel 8:12 ESV). Did you catch the word "elders"? Those are the leaders of the nation. If the Enemy can ensnare or tie up a leader, those under his care are much more vulnerable to attack. If he can destroy the pastor of a church, the members will flee. If the devil can bind a father, the kids and wife are easy prey.

The Bible compares sexual desire to fire. Fire is powerful and can be of great benefit when it burns in the right place, like when it is used to cook our food or provide us with warmth. At the same time, fire can be a most destructive force when it burns out of control, such as when a forest fire devastates the mightiest of trees.

Proverbs warns us: "There are . . . things that are **never** satisfied, . . . [and one of them is] fire, which **never says, 'Enough!'"** (Proverbs 30:15–16 NIV). How true! The more you feed a fire, the hotter it burns. The same is true with lust. Lust is **never** satisfied. The more you feed it, the more it craves.

Another consequence of porn addiction is that it is not easy to overcome. It is a lot like sticky clay. Have you ever been stuck in wet, sticky mud? I will never forget the time we went fishing by a river and sunk into mud up to our knees. I tried to pull one foot out, but my foot popped out of my shoe—the rubber boot was still stuck deep in the clay. I was left balancing on one rubber-booted foot, stuck in the mud, with the other foot bent up behind me like a stork!

We read about Jeremiah's similar experience when the king was angry with his prophecy: "They took Jeremiah and cast him into the cistern. . . . And there was no water in the cistern, but only mud, and Jeremiah sank in the mud" (Jeremiah 38:6 ESV). Poor Jeremiah was later found and rescued, but it took thirty men to overcome the incredible suction that held Jeremiah down and to pull him out of that sticky mud. So great was the force that pulled on Jeremiah that rags had to be thrown down to him to cushion the ropes under his arms.

Porn is just like that sticky mud; it does not let go easily! According to another scientist, there is a chemical reason why porn is so difficult to overcome:

When porn enters the brain, it triggers the reward center to start pumping out dopamine, which sets off a cascade of chemicals including a protein called Delta FosB. Delta FosB's regular job is to build new nerve pathways to mentally connect what you're doing (i.e. the porn you watch) to the pleasure you feel. Those strong new memories outcompete other connections in the brain, making it easier and easier to return to porn.

In other words, **porn rewires your brain!** It literally creates new pathways of memories and thoughts that take over your mind. More than two thousand years ago, God revealed to Jeremiah this rewiring of our neural pathways in the brain: "The sin of Judah is written with a pen of iron; with a point of diamond it is engraved on the tablet of their heart" (Jeremiah 17:1 ESV).

Just as the Ten Commandments were engraved on tablets of stone, the prophet Jeremiah speaks of sins being engraved on the tablets of our hearts and minds. "To engrave" means to etch deeper and deeper grooves into a surface, whether clay, wood, stone, or metal. Each time people return to the same addictive behavior, they create deeper and deeper grooves and ruts that make that behavior easier to repeat.

But here is the good news: if shameful sins can be written in our thoughts, then it is also possible to re-write good, pure, and holy things in our thoughts that can erase and replace the previous evil habits. David gives us hope: "He also brought me up out of a horrible pit, out of the **miry clay**, and set my feet upon a rock" (Psalm 40:2 NKJV).

Here's how we can begin the process of breaking an addiction:

- Replace impure media with Scripture: "**How** can a young man keep his way **pure**? By guarding it according to your **word**. . . . I have stored up your word in my heart, that I might not sin against you" (Psalm 119:9, 11 ESV).
- Renounce all previous involvement with immoral materials. Give back to God the ground you gave to the Enemy.
- Find an accountability partner—someone you trust to **share** your failures with. "Two people are better off than one, for they can help each other succeed. If one person falls, the other can reach out and help. But someone who falls alone is in real trouble" (Ecclesiastes 4:9–10 NLT). Why do we need others to help us? Because porn will not let you go easily! Accountability pulls us out of the mud.
- Install a **software app** that guards you. Try Net Nanny, Covenant Eyes, or another good program.
- Rewire your brain! **Renew** your mind by **meditating** on Scripture: "Let the words of my mouth

and the meditation of my heart be acceptable in Your sight, O Lord, my rock and my redeemer" (Psalm 19:14 ESV).

- Be consistent in reading Scripture. All habits, good or bad, are strengthened by constant repetition. Get an app or a plan that motivates you to read the entire Bible in a year! Consistently reading passages of Scripture has a "washing" effect on our thoughts.
- If you are still struggling, do a Google search on Dr. Doug Weiss. Dr. Weiss has some powerful literature and advice, as well as an online accountability program, that can help you further in this ongoing battle.

Remember, before the devil can attack your family, he first has to bind the strong man (Luke 3:27). That's you, Dad. Be strong in the Lord!

CHAPTER 12:

The Power of Encouragement

Pleasant words are like a honeycomb,
sweetness to the soul and health to the bones.
Proverbs 16:24 NKJV

Do you ever feel like you just can't motivate your teenager to do anything?

Fear not, brave parent. This is common with teenagers who are passing from childhood into young adulthood. They are still discovering their identities and the reasons why certain things are important in life. Keep in mind, however, that what is important to you as a parent is not always important to them.

How can we motivate good or desired behavior in the life of our children?

In order to impress upon our children the values that are truly important, it is vital to first understand how motivation works.

There are two basic ways we can motivate our children:

(1) by using outward pressure and concrete discipline, or (2) by inspiring them from within to make wise decisions on their own. Of course, a child's life begins with the concrete discipline of a parent who initially makes all the decisions for an infant or small child. However, our goal as parents is to enable and equip the child to grow into maturity. To do this, we must shift from making all the decisions for the child to teaching them how to make wise decisions on their own.

Let's examine the first method of motivating our child. We can begin to modify our child's behavior with rules and direct consequences for breaking those rules. This concrete approach works best in the early, formative years of a child's life, but it is important to recognize that this method is limited, as it only affects their outward actions and not their inward attitudes or intentions.

Allow me to illustrate this with a story of a little boy misbehaving in church. Right in the middle of the pastor's sermon, the bored little boy stood up on his chair and started jumping up and down. His embarrassed mother whispered for him to sit down. With a mischievous grin on his face, the boy retorted, "No."

The exasperated mother hissed through her clenched teeth, "I said sit down NOW!"

In an attempt to see how far he could push back against his mother, the little guy repeated emphatically, "NO!"

Desperate, the mom yanked him by his arm back down into the chair. Thinking that she had won this contest of wills, she whispered to him, "That's what happens when you don't listen to your mom! I will **make** you sit down!"

The little boy answered: "I might be sitting down— but in my heart, I am still standing up!"

This mom may have forced her son's outward actions, but she did not shape the inward intentions of his heart. If this is true with small children, it is even more evident with teenagers who are battling raging hormones and are in the midst of discovering who they are. In this chapter, we will further explore the challenges of bad behavior in our children, as well as look at what kinds of discipline are required to instruct, correct, and inform in order to produce good behavior.

A parent applying external pressure in order to force compliance from their child is like trying to tighten a wide belt around an overweight stomach. It restricts the bulging shape to some degree, and the waist may appear flatter and slimmer, but a constricting belt is far less effective than a better fitting belt or weight loss.

Similarly, we must gradually adjust the ways by which we motivate our children. We need to move away from using outward pressure and the fear of negative consequences to inspiring their hearts from within and teaching them how to willingly choose a wiser path of behavior.

This second and much more effective method of motivation seeks to influence our children's decisions with incentives or rewards for positive behavior rather than with punishment and consequences for negative behavior. Positive motivation affects their inward intentions, helping them to recognize for themselves that there is greater value in making wise choices in life.

In his popular book *The Five Love Languages*, Dr. Gary Chapman speaks of the power of words of affirmation. He compares our need for love to that of a car's need for fuel. Any vehicle, whether big or small, fast or slow, requires fuel to run. Dr. Chapman calls this need for love our "love tank." In order for our relationships with others to function properly, we need fuel from them that fills our love tank. The same is true for our children. He writes:

> Inside every child is an "emotional tank" waiting to be filled with love. When a child really feels loved, he will develop normally, but when the love tank is empty, the child will misbehave. Much of the misbehavior of children is motivated by the cravings of an empty "love tank."[6]

Words of affirmation (I prefer the term "words of encouragement") have a powerful effect in motivating good behavior in our children. These words of encouragement are a potent fuel that fills their love tank.

Just as with expressions of physical affection, parents vary in their degree of comfort in regard to verbally expressing encouragement to their children. Slavic parents are especially cautious about praising their children for fear that it will cause prideful feelings in them. As a result, if the child exhibits good behavior, the parents say nothing verbally in response because they feel that the child simply did what should have been done. But if the child failed to do a good job or performed poorly in some area, those same parents will not hesitate to let their children know! A performance-driven parent will always express their dissatisfaction verbally when the performance does not meet their expectations.

On the other hand, if your children bring home all A's on their report cards, do you let them know how great that is?

"But won't those words of praise go to their head and fill them with pride?" someone might ask.

It is true that we must take every precaution to prevent pridefulness in our children. However, to better understand and avoid this, we must be careful what we praise our children for. If we praise them for things for which they had no choice, such as their natural attractiveness, innate talent, or inherited strength, we do tempt them to swell with pride. They were born with those abilities and characteristics and should not take credit for them. Praising them for what they are not responsible for only leads to pride.

However, when we praise or encourage our children for their good behavior and good choices, such as diligently studying in school, completing homework assignments, or helping their parents with chores in the home, then the verbal praise for completing those tasks will not lead them to pride because we are encouraging and affirming their choices rather than their innate characteristics. Praise for good behavior will reinforce and encourage similar good behavior, as well as motivate them inwardly in their hearts.

You might ask, "What is the biblical basis for this practice of positively encouraging our children?" Good choices such as obedience, loyalty, faithfulness, and kindness are what build our character. In other words, our character is formed by what we **choose** to do with our gifts and abilities in a good and moral way. God reveals this powerful truth to his disobedient people through the prophet Jeremiah:

> Thus says the Lord: "Let not the wise man boast in his wisdom, let not the mighty man boast in his might, let not the rich man boast in his riches, but let him who boasts boast in this, that he understands and knows me, that I am the Lord who **practices** steadfast **love**, **justice**, and **righteousness** in the earth. For in **these things** I delight, declares the Lord." (Jeremiah 9:23–24 ESV)

Praising the character of a child actually reinforces the desire within them to repeat those good choices again.

We see this illustrated in the book of Matthew during the baptism of Jesus Christ: "Then Jesus came from Galilee to the Jordan to be baptized by John. But John tried to deter him, saying, 'I need to be baptized by you, and do you come to me?'" (Matthew 3:13–14 NIV). Jesus corrected John by explaining the reason for His request for baptism: "Jesus replied, 'Let it be so now; it is **proper** for us to do this to **fulfill** all righteousness'" (Matthew 3:15 NIV). Jesus's response tells us of His desire to obey His Father in heaven. The author of Hebrews confirms this: "Although he [Jesus] was a son, he learned **obedience** through what he suffered" (Hebrews 5:8 ESV).

What was the result of this obedience of Jesus at His baptism? There was an audible expression of delight, publicly spoken out loud by the Father in the hearing of those present: "This is my beloved Son, with whom I am well pleased" (Matthew 3:17 ESV). If God the Father could not contain His joy at the obedience of His Son, how much more do we, as earthly fathers, need to express our satisfaction **verbally** (that is, with words) to our children when they do the right thing?

Notice how the heavenly Father expressed three important messages to His Son, Jesus:

- First, the Father publicly confirmed before all those assembled by the river that Jesus was the Son of God.

- Secondly, He told His Son that He greatly loved Him.
- Finally, He expressed satisfaction with His Son. He was pleased by the act of obedience His Son displayed in receiving baptism, and He told Him so!

Do we do this with our children when they obey us—when they satisfactorily complete a job we give them?

Just as His Father praised Him, Jesus in turn encouraged Simon Peter, His disciple, prior to Peter's betrayal of Him:

> Simon, Simon! Indeed, Satan has asked for you, that he may sift you as wheat. But I have prayed for you, that your faith should not fail; and when you have returned to Me, **strengthen** your brethren."
> (Luke 22:31–32 NKJV)

Here we see Jesus encouraging Peter ahead of time, telling him that even though he would soon fail in his witness of Jesus, he would later repent. Jesus further instructed Peter to then go on to strengthen and encourage the other disciples, who likewise ran away in fear during Jesus's arrest.

Jesus also **taught** the power of encouragement in His sermons. In the parable of the talents, when two of the servants diligently labored and doubled their owner's investment, Jesus spoke of the master's joy and response to both of his servants: "Well done, good and faithful servant.... Enter into the joy of your master" (Matthew 25:23 ESV). Notice that the master commends his servants for a job well done. He tells them what happiness that brought to him, and he tells his faithful servants to share in his joy with him.

What could this mean? I believe this is an invitation for the servants to join the master in a celebration or reward of some kind, illustrating how we will one day join Jesus in heaven. Wow—talk about motivation! Heaven is a place of celebration and joy where good deeds and faithful service never go unnoticed.

Let me share one more example of the power of encouragement. This one is a lesson I learned from my earthly father.

This happened right after I began pastoring a fairly large and growing Ukrainian church in New Jersey and after my father had retired from active ministry. I was only twenty-eight years of age, and I was quite confident in my abilities to handle this great responsibility. It was a Sunday morning, and I thought I had prepared a terrific sermon that would electrify the congregation. My father sat in the first pew, as was his custom, to hear his son preach.

To my great embarrassment, the message turned out to be a disaster. God humbled my youthful pride that morning. After the final prayer, I descended from the platform, hanging my head in shame, not wanting to look anyone in the eye. As I passed the first pew, my dad stopped me and said, "Don't worry, Son. That was still a good message."

With my head still hanging in shame, I replied, "You only say that because you're my dad. We both know it was a terrible sermon!" Those words made my dad chuckle, and then he said something that I will never forget: "Maybe so, Son, but I want you to know this—you are a gift from God to me."

I raised my head to see if he meant it, and I saw in his eyes that he really did. At that moment, I didn't care about my failed message or about anything else that other people in the congregation might think about me. My dad was happy that I was his son! Those sincere words of encouragement from my father were fuel for my heart. So many sons long to hear encouraging words like these from their fathers.

Dads, the young hearts of your children are strengthened by your words of encouragement. If you don't know what to say or how to encourage your child, you can use some phrases that Helen Doron suggests in her blog:

Phrases to use when someone has not yet started:
- Give it a try.
- Go for it!
- Why not?
- It's worth a shot.

- What are you waiting for?
- What do you have to lose?
- You might as well.
- Just do it!

Phrases to use when someone is already doing well:
- There you go!
- Keep up the good work!
- Good job!
- Keep it up.
- I'm so proud of you!

Phrases to use when someone is having trouble:
- Hang in there.
- Don't give up!
- Keep pushing.
- Keep fighting.
- Stay strong.
- Never give up!
- Never say die.
- Come on, you can do it!

Phrases to use when someone is facing a hard decision:
- I'll support you either way.
- I'm behind you 100 percent.
- It's totally up to you.
- It's your call.

Best of all, biblical phrases to inspire them:
- Well done. Dad/Mom are so happy you are our son/daughter!
- God has chosen you "for such a time as this."
- God is with you wherever you go!
- I trust you, Son/Daughter.
- I believe in you!
- All that I have is yours.
- We celebrate this happy day![7]

CHAPTER 13:

Asking Forgiveness: Passwords, Pride, and Patience

God opposes the proud but gives grace to the humble.
James 4:6 ESV

On one very busy workday, my daughter, Larissa, came to see me while I was working at my desk. I was under a lot of pressure due to a ministry project deadline.

"Dad! Dad! You have to help me with my college registration!" she said, with the-world-is-ending desperation that only a teenager could manufacture. It was her senior year in high school, and she was preparing to attend college the next fall.

I reluctantly stopped what I was doing and asked her what the problem was.

"My password to register online at the college is not

working!" she said frantically.

Normally my daughter is very computer savvy, so I wondered what the problem could be. We tried the password, and it obviously was not working.

"Did the college give you any other passwords?" I asked her.

"Oh yes, there's also another one!" she replied. "I'll go get it!" Great, I thought. Problem solved. I can get back to my work.

That password didn't work either. Now my patience was wearing thin.

"Larissa! There has to be another password they gave you for this registration site! What is it?" By this time, my voice had elevated considerably to a yell.

"Daddy! I don't know! They didn't give me any other password!" she said, crying now.

"There has to be another password! How is it that you don't have it? They must have given it to you. I don't have time for this!" My patience was now long gone!

Larissa stomped upstairs hurt and angry, and she slammed her bedroom door shut.

I sat in my office chair, and I was also angry. *What just happened?* I asked myself. *How did that escalate into a heated argument so quickly?*

A mix of emotions came over me—anger, impatience, sadness that I had an argument with my sweet daughter, and a guilty conscience. In my heart, I heard a still, small voice tell me, "Go upstairs and ask forgiveness for your anger and impatience."

Part of me resisted, most likely due to male pride. "I am the father, and she should come down and apologize to me!" said the male pride voice.

But the voice of my conscience persisted. "Go upstairs and ask her for forgiveness. It's the right thing to do." I sat there for a few more moments, but I knew I had to go upstairs. This situation needed to be resolved.

Reluctantly, I made my way upstairs and knocked on Larissa's bedroom door. I once read that Billy Graham never barged in on his kids, but always respected their privacy and knocked on their doors. I thought that was very honorable, and I adopted that practice with all my children.

Larissa did not answer. I knocked again. Then I heard the sarcastic answer from my upset daughter: "What?" I could tell that my anger and impatience had hurt her tender feelings.

"Daddy came upstairs to ask your forgiveness," I said in my most humble voice.

"Oh, Daddy!" exclaimed Larissa as she rushed to open the door and hug my neck. She forgave me so quickly and so easily.

Many dads refuse to ask forgiveness from their children—even when they know they are in the wrong—because they think asking forgiveness will cause them to lose respect in the eyes of the child. In actuality, the very opposite is true. The child is amazed that a figure of power and authority can admit fault or wrong. When we as fathers, the heads of our homes, ask forgiveness from our children, it truly is an object lesson for our children about humility and about taking responsibility for wrong words or actions. It is a sign of maturity about how we lead our families.

Fathers, the best lessons we could ever teach our children are by example, by living out in front of them the values and principles we want them to emulate. They do not forget those powerful lessons, and those moments will affect them positively for years to come.

After Larissa and I returned to the computer, I discovered on the college website that there was a third password that she had not yet been issued because it had to be requested online. Problem solved! It just took a little more patience on my part.

Months later, Larissa wrote about this incident for an English writing assignment. She wrote, "Although my dad is not perfect, he always asks forgiveness when he knows that he is wrong. It's such a beautiful quality in him that I love the most! I have the best dad!"

CHAPTER 14:

Being Honest:
The Christmas Chairs

An honest witness tells the truth,
but a false witness tells lies.
Proverbs 12:17 NIV

Our children do not just listen to what we **say**, but they also watch what we **do**. They can become easily discouraged by our Christian faith when they see that our actions as dads do not always match our words. However, we can teach them powerful life lessons when they observe us making difficult decisions that demonstrate sincere faith. One of those powerful life lessons is honesty, and it is best taught by observation rather than by preaching.

Let me share an episode that affected my children's lives, although I did not realize how much it affected them until later.

It was Christmas season, and our family had just moved to the Charlotte area from New Jersey. During the Christmas preparations, I realized that we needed more folding chairs for our table in order to accommodate guests for the holiday.

I took my two boys with me to purchase some chairs; AJ was twelve years old and Luke was ten at the time. We parked in the very busy parking lot of a big office supply store and went inside in search of metal folding chairs. We found some for fifteen dollars each, but they were all metal and too cold to sit on. I then saw some padded metal chairs for twenty-five dollars each, and I thought our guests would enjoy those more. We put four of the chairs, along with some other items, in the shopping cart.

The lines to the cashiers were very long, so we patiently joined a line. Our turn came, and we paid for the four chairs and the other items. When we reached our minivan in the parking lot, I noticed that the total on the receipt was only seventy-five dollars. How was that possible? The four chairs alone were one hundred dollars, and I had also bought about fifty dollars' worth of other items.

"I see! She only charged me twenty-five dollars for all four chairs instead of twenty-five dollars each! I saved seventy-five dollars. That's a lot of extra money for Christmas! Isn't God good?" I told the boys.

Immediately, my conscience pierced me. I knew I

couldn't take those chairs home without making things right and paying full price.

"Boys," I said, "wait here. I have to go inside and pay the rest of the bill." They had been watching me to see what I would do.

"No, Dad," they said. "We are going in with you. This is going to be good!" Those were their exact words!

We trudged back into the crowded store carrying the four chairs and the receipt. The lines were even longer this time, so I approached our cashier from the exit side.

"What's the problem?" she asked, eyeing the chairs.

"There's a mistake on our receipt. You undercharged us. These chairs are twenty-five dollars each, but you only charged us twenty-five dollars for all four."

"No, I didn't," she responded. "They are four for twenty-five dollars."

By now, the entire line of people, in addition to my kids, were all watching this exchange.

I bravely continued. "Ma'am, how can they be four for twenty-five dollars when the all-metal chairs are fifteen dollars each? These are the padded ones, and the sign said twenty-five dollars each!"

With the lines so long, she didn't have any time to investigate further, so she sent us to the store manager, with whom I had the same exchange. The manager insisted that the chairs were four for twenty-five dollars, and I tried to be honest by telling her I was willing to pay the real price. To me, it was a question of integrity.

Do you know what happened next? Exasperated, the manager asked me to take the chairs and leave the store! Not wanting to cause a scene, I did. My boys were snickering at this point, but I said out loud, "Well, Lord, You know how hard I tried to do the right thing. She kicked me out of the store!"

A few days later, I stopped at the store again and went inside to check the price on the chairs. The sign clearly said that the padded chairs were twenty-five dollars each! Oh well; the Lord knows I tried!

My boys never forgot this story. When AJ's senior class was graduating from the public high school in our town, I was asked to be the main speaker for the baccalaureate ceremony. Normally they invite the mayor, the police chief, or a dignitary of importance to address the students, their parents, and all the teachers, but the students voted to ask me, a missionary, to be the speaker. What an honor!

Furthermore, one of the top students of the senior class always introduces the main speaker, and they asked AJ to introduce me. I would never have guessed what AJ was going to say in his introduction speech: "Before you hear my dad speak, I want to tell you what kind of a man he is." AJ then proceeded to tell the whole story of the chairs we bought that Christmas and how I tried to be honest with the cashier and the manager. I was incredibly moved that a simple act of honesty on my part became such an important and inspiring teaching moment for my sons.

After my speech, the entire senior class, along with their parents and the teachers of the public high school in our town, gave me a standing ovation. It was such a touching moment and a significant event in our lives and in our family.

Two years later, when Luke was graduating from the same high school, I was again asked to be the main speaker. It seems as if doing one good thing leads to another good thing. God honors those who honor His Word and keep His commands.

Fathers, God watches over us, but **our children also watch us**—like hawks! They hear what we say, they see what we do, and whether we are aware of it or not, they learn from our example, good or bad. After all, as the saying goes, the apple does not fall far from the tree— and I have found that saying to be true.

Do the right thing. Obey God and listen to your conscience. Be honest in your words and actions. Set a good example for your children, and lead the way so they can follow in your footsteps. There is no guarantee that they will make the same choices that you do, because your children are free to make their own choices, but rest assured that your good example certainly serves as a powerful influence for them now and in the years to come.

CHAPTER 15:

The Best Dad in the Bible

As a father has compassion on his children,
so the Lord has compassion on those who fear him.
Psalm 103:13 NIV

Who do you think would be the best example of a great father in the Bible?

Would it be Job, who prayed for his children every day? Would it be Abraham? Isaac might have had different thoughts about that when he was at Mount Moriah with his father. What about Isaac, who played favorites with his son Esau? Jacob certainly would not agree with that. Would you consider David? Maybe he is not the best example, either.

The apostle Paul was single, so he was not the best father. Peter and the disciples were all busy following Jesus. Who is left? You might be surprised to find him in Luke 15, in one of the most familiar parables of the Bible.

Jesus began the story about this man with these

simple words: "There was a man who had two sons" (Luke 15:11 ESV).

"Wait!" you say. "Isn't that the story about the prodigal son?"

Yes, but it is also a story about a father.

Who is the main character in the story of the lost son? Our attention is usually focused on the boy who left his father's house to recklessly pursue dreams of personal freedom and independence. We see him abandon the safety and protection of his home in order to run away to a foreign country and foolishly waste the inheritance his father gave him. But when we examine the context of the entire chapter, we see that the **father** is actually the subject of this drama, with his two sons occupying the supporting roles.

As the story unfolds, we learn what motivated this once prosperous boy, now reduced to rags, to finally decide to return to his father's house. And what about the father? How did he react to his son's return as a barefoot beggar who spent all the money he had given him? There are some powerful parenting lessons in this poignant story of a father who had two very different sons.

Let's first examine the context of the three parables Jesus tells in Luke 15. The parable of the prodigal son is actually the third of three stories that Jesus told the religious leaders of His day. Jesus told the parables of a lost sheep, a lost coin, and a lost son. All three speak of valuable possessions that were lost and then found again. Jesus told these parables in response to the cutting criticism from the Pharisees, who could not understand why Jesus would reach out to broken people with ruined lives, and why He would visit their homes and eat with them.

These ultra-religious leaders murmured and judged Jesus for associating with the lowest class of people in their society. Being very pious and observant Jews, they were shocked when they saw Jesus, who professed to be a prophet from God, mingle with lowly prostitutes, hated tax collectors, and pagans.

"How can He do that? Doesn't He know what kind of people they are? What kind of prophet eats and drinks with such shameful sinners?"

In response to these criticisms, Jesus told the Pharisees three stories, using very human examples, to help them understand things **from God's perspective**. It was as if He were saying: "Look, did you ever have a hundred sheep and lose one of them? Well, did you go looking for it? Weren't you happy when you found it? And what about money? Did you ever lose your wallet or purse with a lot of money in it? You probably searched everywhere for it, even sweeping the corners of the house and shining a light in all the dark places! How did you feel when you found it? Just a little happy? No! You probably called up your best friends, all ex-cited! Even more precious, what if one of your kids ran away from home? Would you care about that? Of course you would! If he is of age, wouldn't you anxiously wait for him to come to his senses and return home again on his own?"

Who couldn't relate to those experiences? We have all experienced losing something of value, something precious that belonged to us. In these three stories, Jesus spoke of the sadness of people who lost precious possessions, and then He described the incredible joy they experienced when the possessions were found again!

Have you noticed who Jesus is really talking about in these stories? He is talking about Himself! In the parable about the lost sheep, Jesus is telling us that He is the Good Shepherd who cares about searching for His lost and wandering sheep. Jesus basically said to the Pharisees, "If you as shepherds care about a lost sheep, how do you think I feel? I care even more about people who have wandered away from their Creator!"

In the second parable, Jesus hinted at the work of the Holy Spirit when He referred to the light that illuminated the dark corners of the house and revealed the location of the lost coin to the searching woman.

In the story about the father whose son became lost, however, Jesus revealed the **true heart of a father**—that of His own heavenly Father—who patiently waits for His wayward sons and daughters to return to Him.

There is one more thing to note before we dive into this third parable. As with many Scripture verses, there is one interpretation of this passage, but there is more than one application. While it is true that Jesus is using this parable to show the character and qualities of His heavenly Father, there are some beautiful and practical examples here that we earthly dads can follow.

Without further ado, let's examine this wonderful parable and learn the powerful lessons it holds for us fathers. We can also look at the father of the prodigal son and see him as a human father. How did this father respond and react when his wayward son finally returned home? Read on to see some of the insights I gleaned as I meditated on this story found in Luke 15:20–24.

1. A true father "sees" his children.

Notice that even when the boy was still a great distance away, the father "saw him" (Luke 15:20 NIV). I mean he really saw him: he saw the boy's broken-down condition; he saw his son's obvious poverty; he saw that he was walking instead of riding; and he especially saw the direction that his son was heading—back to his father's house!

Do you "see" your children? Do you **really** see them? Do you know their true condition? Sometimes it is obvious, as in the case of this lost son, but other times it is not so visible. Do you know what **direction** your children's hearts are heading? Are they facing toward home or away from home? Do you know what they are going through? Do you know who their friends are? There are always signs you can find if you look for them.

After we moved from Union, New Jersey, to Charlotte, North Carolina, our children went through a time of adjusting to a new school. Our two sons, AJ and Luke, were twelve and ten years old; our daughter, Larissa, was only seven. One day Luke came home from school with a sad, pitiful look on his face. My wife immediately knew that something was wrong.

"Luke, why the long face? What happened in school today?"

"Mom, what is a dirty Yankee?" he asked. Then he broke down and started to cry.

If you are unfamiliar with American history, here is a brief explanation. The northern and southern states of the U.S. fought the Civil War in the 1800s over the issue of slavery, threatening to split the nation in two. During this time, people from the northern states were called "Yankees" by those living in the southern states. Now, many years later, the accents of people who move from the north to the south remain different and noticeable. Southern kids teased the newcomers from the northern states because they sounded different.

We were able to comfort our son about this because we "saw" him and what he was feeling deeply in his heart. Later, Luke became very popular at school because of his involvement in the local sports team, and that helped him to gain the acceptance of his peers. It also didn't hurt that he played on the baseball team that won the state championship of North Carolina for thirteen-year-olds!

2. A true father has compassion for his children.

Jesus revealed His heavenly Father's heart in the next part of verse 20: "His father saw him **and was filled with compassion for him**" (Luke 15:20 NIV).

Notice that there was no condemnation. The father never asked his son, "How did you get into this disgraceful condition? Where is the money I gave you? What did you do to yourself?"

Also notice that there was no punishment for the son's actions. Why not? Discipline is important when our child disobeys, as we discussed in a previous chapter, but in this particular instance, discipline was not necessary. Why not?

The reason is because the results of this young man's poor choices were his discipline. He was hungry because he had foolishly spent the money his father had given him, and now he could not pay for any food. He was dirty because of the job he had been forced to accept among the pigs. In other words, **his own sins punished him**; there was no need for his father to administer further punishment or discipline.

When I was about four or five years old, two of my friends came over to our house to play. We went down into the basement, where my dad had some household items stored—a mirror, some suitcases, and a few cans of paint left over from when we had the exterior of the house painted.

My friends and I decided to open these cans of paint, grab some brushes that were lying around, and add a touch of color to the drab basement walls. It was oil-based paint in a nice mint-green color. We then decided that the suitcases could use a touch of color as well, so we painted them. Then the mirror was next. *Ah, everything looks so much better now*, I remember thinking.

One of us accidently knocked over one of the paint cans, and mint-green paint spread all over the linoleum floor. *Wow—this paint sure is slippery on this vinyl floor!* We then began to "ice skate" on the slippery floor, falling down, twisting, and turning every which way on our backs. It was such fun!

Soon it was time to go back upstairs, and my two friends returned to their homes. I trudged up the stairs and shocked my parents by my appearance—I had mint-green hair, clothing, arms, and legs! It was all over my body, from head to toe. Not only that, but my parents were horrified when they saw our newly redecorated basement. My dad began to threaten me with serious and grave punishment, but first they had to get the green paint off me.

My mom filled the bathtub with hot water and added some mineral spirits, but soap and water could not remove the oil-based paint from my skin. She then poured the entire contents of the two-liter bottle of mineral spirits into the bathwater, and the stubborn paint finally came off—along with several layers of my skin! Oh boy, did that ever burn! In fact, the mineral spirits soaked deep into my skin and gave me a high-grade fever. I had to lie in bed for two days to recover from this painful, burning experience.

Did my parents punish me afterward? No, they did not have to! My sin punished me—severely!

The same principle applies to adults when we make wrong choices in life; the results of our own wrong decisions will punish us. Our heavenly Father looks down upon us with a heart of compassion, and He doesn't want to punish us further. His compassionate heart is already sad that we have hurt ourselves, and He sees when we are truly sorry for what we have done.

3. A true father is "approachable."

The father's action here speaks volumes to me about his approachability: ***"But while he was still a long way off, his father . . . ran to his son"*** (Luke 15:20 NIV). It would have been very easy for the father to stand proudly in the doorway, arms crossed, waiting for his son to crawl to him and beg for forgiveness. After all, just look at the young man! He was filthy, ragged, shoeless, and was missing his gold ring—and I am sure the father must have wondered, *What is that horrible smell?*

Yet Jesus tells us that the father ran to his son. Notice the profoundly touching wording that Jesus used to describe this scene of return: the boy **walked**, but the father **ran**.

Details such as these speak of the father's deep desire to quickly reestablish his relationship with his son. The father ran to the son **first**. There was no scolding, no asking why the boy did this, and no rebuke about his poor condition and the obvious loss of his inheritance. His father simply met him with a heart full of love and compassion, grateful that his son was alive and home.

What is your reaction when your child fails? Can your child share with you their failure without fear of further punishment from you?

My wife and I wanted our three children to know that we were approachable if they ever failed in some area of their life. My wife and I discussed this principle between the two of us first, and then we shared it with our teenage children. They were very surprised when we assured them that we would not reject them should they mess up. Rather, we expressed to them that we wanted to be the first people they called if they ever landed in jail, were involved in an illegitimate pregnancy, or were in any other catastrophe. This in no way meant that we would condone their sinful or illegal behavior, but simply that we would want them to come to us first and that they would know that we would help them pick up the broken pieces of their situation.

Soon after this conversation, we received a phone call in the middle of the night from a boy in the same class as our son. He told us he had been arrested the previous night and was calling from jail. Instead of calling his own father first, he called us to bail him out of jail. It made me very sad to see how afraid he was to call his own father. I am sure it was because he feared how his father would react.

A true father is always approachable.

4. A true father is affectionate.

Next, "his father . . . threw his arms around him and kissed him" (Luke 15:20 NIV).

Every culture has a particular level of comfort in showing affection. As a general rule, southern Europeans are very physically affectionate among their families, whereas the northern Europeans tend to be more reserved in showing physical affection. Slavic people are the exception. Although theirs would be considered a more northern climate, they are unashamed to openly greet their family members and close friends with hugs or kisses.

Psychologist Tiffany Field has discovered that French parents and children touch each other three times as often as their American counterparts—a pattern that continues with age. She explains, "America is what anthropologists call a 'nontactile' society, or one that touches infrequently."[8] When another psychologist, Sidney Jourard, observed rates of casual touch among couples in cafés around the world, he reported the highest rate in Puerto Rico (180 times per hour). One of the lowest rates was in the U.S. (two times per hour).[9] Compared with most cultures, Americans are reluctant to touch.

This was not the case with Jesus and His followers. Jesus allowed His disciple John to lay his head on His chest. Jesus did not protest when more than one woman of questionable reputation kissed His feet or bathed them with tears, wiping them with their hair.

It is no wonder, then, that Jesus described the father in Luke 15 as being very affectionate with his wayward son. Despite the dirt on the young man's body and his filthy clothing reeking of pigs, this father hugged his neck and kissed him repeatedly. If this parable is a description of our heavenly Father, then this astounds me—our heavenly Father does not reject us, even in the midst of our miserable failures. His heart's desire is not to punish us, but rather to hug us, to kiss us, and to redeem us from our sins.

Jesus said to Simon the Pharisee, "You did not give

me a kiss" (Luke 7:45 NIV). Wow! Jesus wanted a kiss of greeting, a sign of tenderness and affection, when He entered someone's home. He contrasted Simon's cold behavior with that of the woman who was forgiven of great sins: "but this woman, from the time I entered, has not stopped kissing my feet" (Luke 7:45 NIV).

I don't know how much affection was shown in your home when you were growing up, but my father's house was a place of warm affection and love, accompanied by lots of hugs and kisses. The smell of my father's favorite Old Spice aftershave lotion still lingers in my memory; as a child, I would crawl up onto his lap and kiss his neck after he shaved. Every time I smell Old Spice, precious memories come flooding back of the pleasant smell and the soft feel of my father's face. As a result, we raised our three children the same way—with lots of physical affection and kisses. To this day, in fact, it is still our customary way of greeting our children, who are now grown adults with children of their own.

Our oldest son, AJ, was the first to leave our home, attending a university two hours away. Our first visit to see him was at a sporting event on his campus. He was the shortstop on the university's baseball team, and this was their first game of the season. As we made our way down the stadium steps, we saw the players on the field warming up. Our son was among his teammates, and I remember thinking, *Okay, I won't embarrass him by kissing him in front of his fellow baseball players. I will just shake his hand like the Americans do.*

To my utter surprise, as we approached AJ, he grabbed my hand, pulled me close, and kissed me on the cheek, saying, "Hey Dad, what's the matter? Are you embarrassed to kiss me in front of my friends?"

"No, no, I'm good, Son." I was astonished as his buddies looked on with smiles on their faces.

George Howe Colt, in an article in *Life* magazine, explains the importance of physical touch:

> **Touch is a primal need**, as necessary for growth as food, clothing or shelter. Michelangelo knew this: When he painted God extending a hand toward Adam on the ceiling of the Sistine Chapel, he chose touch to depict the gift of life. From the nuzzles and caresses between mother and infant that form the foundation of the self, to the holding of hands between a son and his dying father that allows a final letting go, **touch is our most intimate and powerful form of communication.**[10]

God created within us this desire and need for physical touch when He formed the first man, Adam. He could have created Adam by speaking him into existence with His words, as He did with the rest of creation, but God formed Adam from the soil of the ground **with His hands**. What a significant detail that speaks of the intimacy of God—that He would use touch as the means of completing His special and final creation!

Additionally, Jesus would often heal the sick by laying His hands on them, as He did with the leper in Mark 1. This poor leper, used to people avoiding him, was not sure that Jesus would heal him. He saw others who had been afflicted with illnesses being healed by the hands of Jesus, but he had contagious leprous ulcers on his body. Who would want to touch those? Yet his desperate condition drove him to cry out to Jesus on his knees:

> "If You are willing, you can heal me and make me clean," he said. Moved with compassion, Jesus reached out and touched him. "I am willing," he said. "Be healed!" (Mark 1:40–41 NLT)

Can you imagine what it felt like to be touched by Jesus when everyone else avoided physical contact with him because of his contagious disease? Words cannot describe what this simple act of compassion must have felt like to this leper. It is not difficult to imagine him thinking, *Jesus touched me. He actually touched me!*

In the same way, I think the prodigal son must have wept when, despite his filthy condition, he was embraced and kissed by his father. Let us earthly fathers learn this lesson from this parable of Jesus and not be hesitant to express physical affection with our children.

5. A true father raises the self-esteem of his children.

"The father said to his servants, 'Quick! Bring the best robe and put it on him'" (Luke 15:22 NIV). Was this an expression of fashion, or, as many do today, were they seeking a brand name to be prominently shown on their clothing so as to impress everyone? It seems that many people want their fashion choices to proclaim, "See what expensive clothing and accessories I have? Admire me!"

This is not the case here. When Jesus mentioned that the father replaced the young man's filthy clothing with a new garment, He was speaking of the spiritual transformation we undergo when God removes the dirty garments of our sin and replaces them with a new, clean, white robe of righteousness.

There is an additional lesson here that earthly fathers can learn from this in regard to their children: **how to raise their self-esteem**. Allow me to explain.

One of the many consequences of sin is that it causes us to lower our perception of self-value when we fail. A downward spiral begins when we are tempted to sin by the devil and then give in to sinful choices. As a result, we feel shame and failure, and then we further descend into self-rejection. Adding to these feelings of self-loathing, the Enemy whispers to us: "Look how far you have fallen! You are dirty; you are garbage! Who wants you now? You are a failure! You might as well go all the way!" The Enemy attempts to drive us even deeper into sin by using our feelings of poor self-worth against us.

Jesus speaks directly against those feelings by raising our perception of how valuable we are to God: "For what does it profit a man to gain the whole world and forfeit his soul?" (Mark 8:36 ESV). Our soul is more valuable than all of the riches and treasures in the entire world. We are not garbage; we are precious in God's eyes, despite our poor choices. God's goal is to redeem us, to promote our value, and to bring us to the place of self-respect once again—and this is what the father putting a new, clean robe on his son represents.

The robe also illustrates a delicate balance between two extremes of human behavior. One extreme is the pride and vainglory of seeking exclusive clothing so as to be admired by others. The other extreme is the mistaken understanding that we have to wear drab and unadorned clothing as a sign of humility or spirituality. We must reject both of these false understandings and instead see how **God** views beauty.

The place that Jesus calls "my Father's house" is a place of extraordinary beauty and value. God used the most precious materials in the construction of the new Jerusalem, the capital city of heaven. The gates are made of pearl, the very streets are purest gold, and the foundations of the city are twelve precious stones of dazzling and varying colors (Revelation 21:19-21). We are also told what clothing awaits us in heaven: "The wedding of the Lamb has come, and his bride has made herself ready. Fine linen, bright and clean, was given her to wear" (Revelation 19:7–8 NIV). There is no vainglory or pride in heaven, though, but only **beauty** and **purity** of heart. This is key to understanding why Jesus spoke of the father calling for the "best robe" to replace the damaged clothing of his repentant son.

I believe that the robe was mentioned to make a statement, but it might not be the statement we would expect wearing a fine garment would convey. The message of the father to his son by the robe might have been something like this: "Son, you are still dear to me. You have value in my eyes, and I want you to know that you are worthy of respect and honor in my house." The father called for the **best** robe in order to raise his son's self-esteem and self-worth when he was at his lowest point.

So how does this apply to us fathers today? My father instilled in us a healthy understanding that, as his children, we should always show respect in our manner of dress before others, before ourselves, and especially in God's house. After all, we put on our best clothing for a formal occasion like a wedding, a graduation, or a job interview. Would you go to those formal occasions in a torn T-shirt, ragged shorts, and flip-flop sandals? Think about that for a moment. Why not, then, dress more appropriately in God's house?

Let me emphasize again that the goal is not to show off. Rather, we should raise our self-respect and **honor others** with our apparel from a truly humble and pure motive. The appropriate clothing boosts our self-esteem and shows due respect for those around us. I understand that we live in a casual age where comfortable clothing is accepted, but if you wouldn't go to the White House dressed casually, why would you go to God's house dressed that way?

At a very formative time in my life, God called me to attend Bible school. I met many young men there who had recently been saved out of a culture of drugs. They had not been brought up in church as I had been. They did not have much nice clothing.

God spoke to me about giving away some of my better clothing to them. At first, it was hard to part with my favorite shirts and pants, but I discovered that giving away what you love actually enriches your soul. This became such a blessing to me that I returned home at the end of the school year with just one pair of pants and two shirts.

My dad soon noticed that I returned home with much less than I had left with, and he asked me where my clothing had gone. Now that I think about it, maybe he was worried that I was going to start dressing like those in the hippie drug culture of the day!

Instead, my father took me by train from New Jersey to New York City and bought me a very nice new suit. It was very expensive for his meager salary as a pastor, but it became my favorite suit. More than a very generous gift from my father, it was also a lesson that showed me how much he wanted me to dress respectably. I still remember his exact words to me: "Propovidnyk maye harno vyhlyadaty!" ("A preacher has to have a nice appearance!") Yep. That was my Tato (Dad).

My wife and I passed this concept on to our children, and they, in turn, are dressing their little ones in the same way—not extravagantly or pridefully, but to show honor to others and to promote self-respect and self-worth.

6. A true father motivates his children to achieve by sharing his authority.

In addition to the robe, "The father said to his servants, . . . 'Put a ring on his finger'" (Luke 15:22 NIV).

What was the significance of this ring? Author John Martin writes:

> It was the granting of authority to a person. Whoever has such a ring has the power of attorney for his master. He has authority, his master's authority, to make decisions and to help the master govern his kingdom. And [in Luke 15], when the father places the ring on the hand of his

son, he not only welcomes him back home as a son, but he welcomes him back to responsibility and authority.[11]

We see this custom in the book of Genesis when Pharaoh appointed young Joseph as second ruler over the land of Egypt. As proof of this authority, Pharaoh gave him his signet ring. This ring was more than jewelry; it was a royal symbol to everyone in the kingdom of Egypt that Joseph was granted the great responsibility of sharing in Pharaoh's rule.

How can we fathers teach responsibility to our children? What are some ways that we can share our authority with them?

My father taught me shared authority in my teenage years when he was the pastor of a growing Ukrainian congregation in New Jersey. As a new immigrant to the U.S., his English was limited, so he preached his sermons in Ukrainian. At the same time, our congregation had a younger generation who had been born in the U.S. and were increasingly in need of his messages being translated into English.

In order to address this need, my father had me stand beside him in the pulpit on Sundays and translate his sermons from Ukrainian to English. This was not difficult for me because I was born in America and English was my first language. Due to the fact that my parents spoke very little English, I had learned

Ukrainian at home.

My father was an excellent preacher and was in demand as a speaker. He was invited to preach at many neighboring churches, as well as at large conferences. If he had to speak to American or Canadian congregations, he took me along to translate his words into English. It was a wonderful learning experience for me, as I soon realized that people listening only understood **my words** as I translated my father's Ukrainian into English. That experience served as a powerful lesson of how my father shared his authority with me, and it allowed me to mature and develop greater responsibility in my own ministry.

As a result, I gained a more extensive vocabulary in the Ukrainian language, and I gained deeper insight into the Scriptures as I translated my dad's words. I learned by example how to preach, listening to my father's phrasing of words and his sermon construction. Soon I knew all of his stories and illustrations—even before he told them. It was a wonderful apprenticeship.

When I became a father, I wanted to implement this principle of granting authority to my three children. In the same way that my father took me along with him on his trips, I took each of my children with me on my mission trips to Ukraine, the birthplace of their paternal grandparents. Rather than take them together as a group, I thought that taking them separately would be more special and meaningful for them.

Since AJ was the oldest, he was the first to accompany

me to Ukraine. We visited churches, sang at stadiums, and then brought a team to serve at some orphanages. AJ, only sixteen at the time, wrote of his experience:

> This missions outreach to Ukraine was the greatest experience of my life. It allowed me to travel to a poor country and share the gospel with them.
>
> At the concerts and stadiums, people were so ready to receive Christ that when my father gave the altar call, they came rushing forward to give their lives to the Lord. In Ukraine, they are unashamed to demonstrate their new faith publicly. That was such an inspiration to us all.
>
> Working with the orphans was yet another great experience. We were sad when we saw the broken-down conditions of the place. When the little children, ages three to five, came outside to meet us, they were so cute and friendly. Without a bit of fear, they jumped up into our arms. All of us held the kids and had fun tickling them. I really can't tell you the emotions we all felt—very moving to say the least.
>
> We bought paint and some carpentry tools to refurbish broken-down slides and teeter-totters. The swing set had a pole across the top, but no

swings. Now they will have swings that our team brought from home. Small things I guess, but for God's children, a gift of immeasurable worth. We painted much of the facility and cleaned up the yard to allow them more room to play outdoors.

I will remember this trip for the rest of my life!

These experiences made such a deep impression on my son that he later shared them with other athletes when he was a university student and served as one of the leaders of the Fellowship of Christian Athletes chapter on his college campus.

Sharing my authority with my other son, Luke, was also a blessing for me, as well as a big surprise. This happened when I decided to record new music for a CD in English. Normally my music is for the Slavic community and is recorded in the Ukrainian language. Our music has been recorded over a period of fifty years (yes, you read that correctly—our first recorded song, "Isus Z Nazaretu," was in 1969, and our first album, *Nebesna Krayina*, was recorded at the end of 1970).

In preparation for the new English CD, I asked Luke to pick one song that he really liked, telling him that he could sing that song on the CD. He told me that he couldn't decide between three songs that he liked, and he asked if I could help him choose. All three were very different, but I actually liked all three also.

"Okay, Luke. How about you sing all three?"

He was thrilled, and he was even more excited when I took him with me to record our CD in one of the best studios in Nashville, Tennessee, where many country artists record their music. The musicians we hired played for all the well-known country singers. The large recording studio was amazing and was equipped with the latest and best recording equipment. Luke just stared at all of this with eyes as big as saucers.

I had Luke enter the isolated recording booth to sing our first song. The normal vocal recording process requires the singer to first record what are called the "scratch vocals." Scratch vocals are recorded when the singer sings a song for the first time so the musicians can listen to it and become familiar with it as they follow along on the written musical score for their instrumental parts. It usually takes two or three passes of the vocalist singing the entire song all the way through in order for the musicians to get it perfect. At that point, a red button is pushed and the song is recorded. The purpose of this first recording is for the musicians to "lay down" their individual parts on separate music tracks. The scratch vocal is later erased and the singer re-records his vocal track.

The scratch vocal is never used as the final version because, at a later date, the singer puts on headphones and listens to the music already recorded, and then he can record multiple takes until he finally achieves a satisfactory result.

Luke surprised us all because his very first time recording the scratch vocal was perfect! Listening to it later while doing the final mix, we realized that it was so fresh and full of heartfelt emotion that we used the scratch vocal as the final version without any changes. It became the title song of our CD called "*I Will Follow*": *The Davidiuks Version 2.0.* You can download it on iTunes or Amazon.

I always knew Luke had a very sweet voice, but I was truly surprised to hear his hidden talent. As a result, I asked him to record the lead voice on two more songs on that CD project because I discovered that his vocals are much better than mine!

When you share your authority with your children, don't be surprised if you discover that their gifts can far surpass yours—but that is a wonderful discovery to make as a father.

Larissa was sixteen when she accompanied me on her first trip to Ukraine. Here is what she wrote after her trip:

> I went on my first mission trip to Kyiv, Ukraine, with my dad and six other young people from America.
>
> We visited an orphanage called "Father's House" and went to their summer camp facility. There

were about sixty children there. We decorated some T-shirts that we brought for all the children and did fun activities with them. One of our boys brought six professional soccer balls donated from his college team in the U.S.

All of the children were so thrilled with all of the attention we gave them. I'm sure they never felt so much love in their entire lives!

So many of them used to be street children, living in basements and sewers. Others were abused by alcoholic parents. When you looked into their eyes, you could see brokenness and hurt. It was so hard to say goodbye to them. They hugged us so hard, like they never wanted to let us go.

We saw souls saved, orphans ministered to, and God's work accomplished. I am thrilled that I could be a part of what God is doing in Ukraine!

As a father, I was so happy to see Larissa demonstrate her ability to communicate well with others in the churches we visited in Ukraine. Before I would preach the final message in each church, we would ask one of the team members to give a brief testimony as part of our program. When it was Larissa's turn, she spoke about when Jesus said that we are "the light of the world." On that day, I saw her ability to articulate her words and communicate very effectively to a large crowd. Again, I was pleasantly surprised to discover how well our children can do when we share our authority with them.

Now as a grandfather of eight small children, I can't wait to take my grandkids with me on a mission trip some day!

7. A true father teaches grace over law.

Here is the third piece of the son's transformation: "The father said, 'Quick! . . . Put . . . sandals on his feet" (Luke 15:22 NIV).

Have you ever wondered why the prodigal son returned home barefoot? Was it because his sandals were ruined in the mud with the pigs? Did they tear from overuse? Did the young man lose them?

None of the above. We get a hint about what happened to them from the particular phrasing used to describe how the young man found work tending pigs for the farmer: "He [the lost son] went and **joined himself** to a citizen of that country, and he [the farmer] sent him into his fields to feed swine" (Luke 15:15 NKJV).

No one walked around barefoot in Jesus's day except slaves, and the Greek word for "joined" in this verse has the meaning of being glued or stuck. In other words, the prodigal son was without freedom or independence; he sold himself as a slave to the farmer. He was barefoot because the master would take away the sandals from his slaves to make it harder for them to run away. Furthermore, no Jewish boy would ever voluntarily care for pigs unless he was forced to do so as a slave.

Imagine that! The son of a wealthy father sold himself to be a slave!

That is why his father immediately reacted when he saw his son returning home barefoot: "My son is not someone's slave; he is my **son**!"

This illustrates two contrasting positions or stations in life: that of a slave and that of a son. Paul, in his letter to the Galatian church, describes this stark contrast to us:

> Abraham had two sons, one by the **slave** woman and the other by the **free** woman. His son by the slave woman was born according to the flesh, but his son by the free woman was born as the result of a divine promise. These things are being taken figuratively: The women represent two covenants. (Galatians 4:22–24 NIV)

Paul is describing to the Galatian church that the son of promise, Isaac, represents **grace**, and the son of a slave woman, Ishmael, represents **law**.

How does that relate to us as fathers? Let me use two simple expressions that describe both law and grace: **"have to"** versus **"want to."**

In the very young years of a child's life, the parent must influence most of the decisions in the child's life: you **have to** eat your vegetables, you **have to** brush your teeth, you **have to** clean your room, and so on. As our children mature, our methods of bringing them to maturity must be adjusted accordingly. Our goal is to teach them to be self-motivated so that they would **want to** make proper and healthy decisions in life, willingly and by their own **choice**.

"Want to" decisions are voluntary. They arise from a person's inner motivation, fueled by understanding, wisdom, and maturity, as opposed to an outward obligation that is forced upon them.

My wife and I decided to make a change in our children's lives during their last year at home before they went away to college. We did this same thing for all three of our children during their senior year of high school.

Knowing that many young people are overwhelmed by the sudden rush of complete freedom during their first year of college, away from the watchful eyes of their parents, we wanted our children to experience this freedom gradually rather than all at once. I discussed a radical idea with my wife that some parents might view as risky or unnecessary. The following approach might not work with every child, but we were confident enough that our children were ready to accept this new responsibility. I said to my wife:

What if we took away the curfew from our sons and daughter during their senior year of high school? They can choose to come home any time they wish. After all, they can do this next year at college anyway, so why not get them adjusted to this new freedom while they are still here at home?

My wife looked at me funny at first, but later agreed. We also added a few conditions for safety reasons. Our children had to tell us where they were and who they were with, they had to carry a cell phone with them, and they had to go to school the next morning no matter how little sleep they had.

Do you know what we discovered? Once your children can stay up as late as they want to with your permission, they no longer want to stay up late! Their common sense brings them home at a decent hour so they can get a good night's sleep. None of our children ever abused this privilege of grace, whether at home or later at college. **"Want to"** works much better in your child's heart than **"have to."**

Notice that the prodigal son came home **voluntarily**. In the first parable in Luke 15, the sheep was lost and did not know the way home. The good shepherd found it and carried it home on his shoulders. The coin was also lost, but obviously it was not alive, so it did not even know it was lost. The son, however, **knew** that he was lost, and he also knew the way home. It was only when he came to his right mind that he made the choice to **willingly** return to his father's house.

Once again, **"want to"** is so much more effective than **"have to."**

There is one more observation I want to mention, this one about the word "grace." Grace can be defined in several ways, but the verse that best describes how it works in our Christian lives is Philippians 2:13(NLT): "For God is working in you, giving you the desire and the power to do what pleases him [His will]."

This verse tells us that God's grace consists of two things: (1) The **desire** to do His will and (2) the **power** to do His will. Whether it is the salvation of our soul or the energy to continue living the Christian life, God's grace is what empowers us. Let's break that down.

Ephesians 2:5 tells us that we are saved by grace. What does that mean? There was a time in each of our lives when we had no desire for God. We lived our own lives in whatever way we thought best. Yet God loves each person with such an incredible love that He gently tugs on our heart to seek Him—to know Him not only as our Creator, but also as our heavenly Father, and to know His Son, Jesus Christ.

If we respond to that inner prompting of our heart, we are responding to the grace of God that gives us the desire to know Him—but that is not enough to save us from the power of sin that so easily wraps us up in its grip. We need the power of God to break sin's hold on us. That is what grace does. We humbly ask Him to forgive us for our sin, and we rely on His power for strength to further live as believers in His Son.

Let me share with you a very human example that took place in our home that will illustrate this powerful truth. One day in December, as we were preparing for Christmas, I noticed my ten-year-old daughter, Larissa, sitting on the sofa and quietly crying. "What's wrong, Larissa?" I asked, concerned.

"The boys [her older brothers] have jobs, and they bought you a Christmas present. I'm just a little girl, and I have no money to buy you a present," she said, as hot tears coursed down her face. My heart was touched by her generous desire to give me a gift for Christmas, and I reached in my wallet and gave her a twenty-dollar bill.

"Here, Larissa," I said. "Take this money and go with Mommy to the mall. You can buy Daddy a little black flashlight that he needs for his trips." She accepted my provision gratefully, and on Christmas morning she presented me with a little box nicely wrapped with a bow.

As I opened it, I tried to show surprise, and I said, "A black flashlight! Thank you, Larissa! Just what I needed!"

You see, my daughter had a desire to "do my will"—that is, she wanted to please me, but she had no power—no money—to do what I asked. So I, the father who loves his little girl, gave her the power, the money, to do what I asked her to do for me. That's grace. That is what God wants to do in your life as well. Our heavenly

Father knows that we sometimes lack either the desire or the power to do what we know is His will. If we would only humble ourselves and acknowledge that we don't have the ability to live the Christian life without His divine grace, and when we humbly ask Him as our Father, God will give us the grace that will provide both the "want to" and the "power to do so."

The condition? Humility: "God resists the proud, but gives grace to the humble" (James 4:6 NKJV).

8. A true father celebrates life with his family.

The father wasn't finished yet. He was pulling out all the stops for his son: "The father said . . . 'Bring the fattened calf . . . Let's have a feast and celebrate'" (Luke 15:22–23 NIV).

What day of the week was it when the son returned home? Was it on a special holiday when all work had ceased and the entire household was eating and celebrating? More likely, it was a normal weekday, a day like any other. The day was made special because a son who was lost had returned to his father's house. Imagine his father's joy! No one but a parent could ever understand just how emotional this occasion was. A son who was estranged was now reunited with family again!

I love this last detail of Jesus's parable. It speaks of the joy and celebration that takes place in heaven when a sinner turns to God. In fact, all three of the parables that Jesus told in Luke 15 end with the head of the household expressing great joy that was freely shared with neighbors.

Jesus was hinting about the very first thing that will happen after His second coming and we are all finally gathered together—we are invited to a celebration feast: "'Blessed are those who are invited to the wedding supper of the Lamb!'" (Revelation 19:9 NIV). Jesus told His disciples at the Last Supper, "I tell you I will not drink again of this fruit of the vine **until that day** when I drink it new with you in my Father's kingdom" (Matthew 26:29 ESV). That day will be a wonderful and joyous celebration. It will be a great reunion with those who have died before us; we will see them again and will be together for eternity. What an amazing realization: God is an emotional, loving Father who joyfully prepares a banquet for His Son, Jesus, and His Bride, the church! That's us!

Another exciting detail to this story is that food and drink will be served, just as they would be on any other special occasion. I don't think this mention of food in heaven is a figure of speech or a metaphor. It will be real food, and it will be delicious food, as anything God does has to be excellent.

The happiest occasions in the Bible always seem to center around a dinner table, whether it is a beggar being invited to King David's table, or Jesus knocking on our door and asking to sit at the table with us. The food is not the best part, though; the best part is the **celebration of family** and the loving relationships around the table. The food is just an added benefit.

Nevertheless, Jesus tells us that His Father's house is a place of great celebration. This brings us to the final application of this story for fathers.

Are our homes places where we celebrate with our children? That is a simple question, and I want to share what we have done in our home with our children.

Every single birthday of our three young children was a celebratory event. On each of their birthdays, we would invite their friends and playmates over for food and fun activities. We always had a cake and candles and tried to make the time creative and special. Christmas and Easter were also huge events in our family! They were times of celebrating Jesus's birth and resurrection. There were always nicely wrapped gifts under the Christmas tree, I would take my guitar and we would sing carols, and one of the children would read the Christmas story out loud.

For Easter, Esty always made three Easter baskets for the kids with fun little gifts and chocolate! This practice continued throughout their time in college. They would eagerly wait to receive those baskets in the mail! We also tried to wear our nicest clothes for that Easter Sunday. That is celebration! Family and food together!

But there was one particular birthday celebration

that I can never forget. It happened to be my birthday celebration, but that was not the most important thing about it.

We were living in Charlotte then. It was in May, around the time our future son-in-law, Isaac, began a relationship with our daughter, Larissa. We decided to take everybody to a really nice restaurant to celebrate.

I want to make something clear. We don't like to waste money, especially on a minister's budget. Yes, it is much cheaper to cook at home and save money, but I consider the occasional time eating out as a very special occasion and as an investment in my family and wife. My wife gets a break from cooking and cleaning up afterward, and we can relax and enjoy the time together. Okay, back to the story.

We ate the first course, which was cheese fondue. The plates were cleared, and as we waited on the second course, I had an idea. I said, "This is a special time that we are together. Can we go around the table and speak of one positive quality that you see in a family member that you want to praise?"

We did this for each family member, starting with my wife and ending with me. One by one, each of our grown children praised Esty for having a servant's heart. We did the same for the next person. Soon, tears started to flow as words of affirmation touched each heart. It was such a time of heartfelt emotion and sharing of what we appreciated in each other.

Then it was my turn to hear words of affirmation. My heart was filled with deep emotion as I heard my future son-in-law tell me with tears in his eyes, "You are the most generous person I have ever met!" He was the newest addition to our family, and he was just learning about us.

Then my daughter, Larissa, recounting the time I helped her through a difficult period in her life, said to me, "Daddy, your words to me at that time were like the words of Jesus." Wow! I was undone. Her words touched the deepest core of my heart. What an evening of celebrating family—sitting around a table together, not only sharing great food, but also sharing incredible love and heartfelt conversation!

To me, that is what celebration is about.

You only get one life, fathers.

Make it count.

Make it special for your family.

Celebrate what you have with those you have.

Jesus does! He is eagerly waiting to very soon drink that cup with us around His table!

CHAPTER 16:

The Privilege to Bless

The blessing of the Lord be on you;
we bless you in the name of the Lord.
Psalm 129:8 NIV

Did you know that when you become a father, God gives you a special ability to bless your children? What do I mean by that? How does that work?

We read in Genesis about the last moments of the patriarch Jacob before he died:

> All of these are the twelve tribes of Israel [Jacob's twelve sons]. This is what their father said to them as he blessed them, blessing each one with the blessing **suitable** to him." (Genesis 49:28 ESV)

We learn from this passage of Scripture that there is one more thing Jacob must do before he passes away from this earth: he must pray a blessing over each of his twelve sons. One by one, each of his sons approached the bed on which their aging father lay. As Jacob placed his hands upon the head of each of his sons, the Bible tells us that he blessed each one of them with a "suitable" blessing. That means he prayed a specific prayer tailored to the needs and to the exclusive destiny of each of his sons. Having done that, Jacob was then able to draw his last breath in peace.

Is this act of blessing something that was done only in the Old Testament? Does it have relevance for fathers today? My answer is yes, this does have relevance for fathers today!

Look at what Jacob declared:

> Your father's blessings are **greater** than the blessings of the ancient **mountains**, than the bounty of the age-old hills. Let all **these** [Jacob's blessings] rest on the head of Joseph, on the brow of the prince among his brothers. (Genesis 49:26 NIV)

Here the patriarch compares the blessings of a father to ancient mountains and age-old hills—symbols of strength, magnificence, and endurance. Yet Jacob goes on to declare that the blessings of our father are even greater than these mountains! It is critical that every father should realize this simple truth: your power to bless your children is greater than the strength and majesty of mountains.

To bless means to empower, or to delegate authority and strength. In the case of Jacob with his sons, it also conveyed a sense of affirming their identity to help them recognize who they are as individuals. Part of the blessing of a father is to instill the understanding that each of his children are unique, that they are gifted in a particular area or field and are equipped to succeed in life and to be a blessing to others by utilizing their gifts well. They can use their God-given gifts positively, wisely, and beneficially, or they can choose to use them selfishly and misuse those strengths for selfish purposes.

It is also important to note that fathers are not the only ones who can extend this blessing, but **leaders** can also motivate their followers, **teachers** can inspire their students, and **mentors** can do much to shape the lives of those who are under their influence. Nevertheless, I believe **fathers** wield the greatest power and influence to shape the lives of their children simply because their children grow up in their homes and observe their lives.

There is no question that mothers also shape the lives of their children in a very powerful way, but I want to point out that **fathers** give distinct identity to their **sons**. A boy learns what it means to be a man by watching and observing his father. A daughter learns from her father what a man of character looks like and what to look for in a future husband. She receives appropriate affection from a warm and loving father, and she is not "love starved." She won't desire to seek love in the arms of a boy who might take advantage of her need for affection.

Sadly, this blessing of the father is too often missing in our day of single-parent homes where the father is absent and the mother has to struggle alone to raise her family. In the absence of a father, a boy can still be positively influenced if he has a caring older brother who looks out for him, or if he has a mentoring coach or teacher at school. He can also be greatly influenced by a leader at church whom he looks up to. In the absence of a father, these male figures can often help to supplement a boy's idea of manhood.

How can fathers use their influence to practically extend blessings to their sons and daughters? I experienced this growing up in my father's house, and it became much clearer to me after his death. In the days and weeks after his funeral, I began to contemplate how much my father had influenced my life with his prayers, his faith, and his teachings. I want to share with you this particular area of his blessing that has been formed in me.

The Laying of Hands upon Our Children

The blessing of children by their father is in the power that comes from the laying of his hands upon his children.

Notice that Jacob physically laid his hands on the head of his sons to bless them, and he did so once again on Joseph's sons, Manasseh and Ephraim.

My dad did this with me on numerous occasions when I was a young boy. Although he was my dad, he was also Pastor Andrew Davidiuk, the shepherd of the Ukrainian Assembly of God church in Newark, New Jersey. On Sunday mornings, the church was filled to capacity, but it was on Sunday nights, when there were fewer people present, that my dad would call people forward to the altar for prayer.

One of my favorite memories of these evenings was kneeling in a corner of the altar area and praying with one eye closed, while my other eye was watching my dad go around praying for the other people there. Inevitably, he would come around to me, and I would tightly close both eyes and pray more fervently! I still remember the gentle touch of his hands upon my head and the powerful surge of God's presence on me.

My father laid his hands on my head and prayed over me many times throughout my life, including on my wedding day and on the day of my ordination as pastor of our church. Another occasion that stands out to me was the time we visited his house after our honeymoon. We had just moved into our own apartment, and we went over for our first visit with my parents as a married couple. After a pleasant time of conversation, I said to my dad, "Tato, you blessed us on our wedding day, but I was wondering if you could lay your hands on our heads and bless us in our new lives together."

His kind eyes grew brighter. "Of course!"

My wife and I knelt on the green carpet in my father's house, and we experienced a powerful blessing as he laid his hands on our heads and prayed for us. Words cannot describe the powerful presence of heaven in the room as he raised his voice to God, asking Him to bless our marriage. We felt such amazing significance in that humble encounter, and I will never forget it.

Soon after that, we flew to Canada to visit Esty's childhood home in Bonnyville, Alberta. We enjoyed seeing her family, and we made sure to visit her paternal grandfather, Dido (Grandpa) Moses Kalinski. He was a widowed pensioner well into his 90s, living in a tiny house in that farming town.

As we entered his tiny home, we saw him sitting at the kitchen table with a huge Ukrainian Bible opened to the book of Psalms. He was so happy that we had come to visit him, but he was even happier that I could speak Ukrainian with him, and we discussed the Scripture passage he was reading.

When the time came for us to leave, the idea occurred to me to ask him to pray for us. "Dido Moses, you are the grandfather of the big Kalinski family. Since I married your granddaughter, you are now my Grandpa too. Can I ask you for something?"

I guess he must have thought that I was hitting him

up for some cash because he reached for his wallet.

"No, Dido, not money. As the oldest Kalinski, you are the patriarch of the Kalinski family. Could you lay your hands on our heads and bless us with the father's blessing?"

I will never forget the expression of surprise on his face as he soberly nodded his head yes.

My new wife and I knelt on that humble kitchen floor as Dido Kalinski laid his aged farmer's hands upon our heads and prayed a powerful prayer of blessing over our lives. Again, words cannot describe the significance of that grandfather's prayer of blessing for Esty and me.

After those two instances of a father's blessing, I wondered to myself, *Why can't more fathers pray these blessings over their children and grandchildren?*

Well, the answer is that they can—and they should! As fathers and grandfathers, we **should** pray them, and as children we should ask for those prayers from our fathers. I believe powerful blessings will result for our children if we simply take the time to ask God to bless them and to direct them to follow His ways.

Someone might protest, "But that only occurred in the Old Testament!"

Let's examine what Jesus did with the small children whom their mothers brought to Him: "They were bringing children to him that he might touch them" (Mark 10:13 ESV). The gospel of Mark tells us that Jesus scolded His disciples when they tried to prevent these children from coming to Him, for they had not realized the importance of an occasion for blessing them. Mark describes what happened next: "He took them in his arms and blessed them, laying his hands on them" (Mark 10:16 ESV). The Son of God teaches us—and shows us—the importance of blessing our children.

The apostle Paul, although single and not a father, nevertheless became a mentor and spiritual father to young Timothy. Paul also illustrates the importance of blessing in the New Testament. He encouraged this young preacher by reminding him to "fan into flame the gift of God, which is in you through the **laying on of my hands**" (2 Timothy 1:6 ESV).

The blessing of a father, whether spiritual or biological, is both biblical and relevant for today. You can bless your children or grandchildren when they are newly born or when they are in their childhood. You can lay hands on them as they sleep. You can bless them on special occasions such as graduations or weddings. You can pick the time and the place, dads, but just do it—and do it often.

CHAPTER 17:

Releasing Your Children

By faith Moses' parents hid him for three months after he
was born, because they saw he was no ordinary child,
and they were not afraid of the king's edict.
Hebrews 11:23 NIV

Letting go is hard. In fact, letting go is even harder than holding on! By nature, we are collectors. We like to possess the things we consider as "ours," and this is especially true with our children.

Mothers in particular are thrilled when a newborn baby comes into their lives for the first time; they love and cherish this miracle of God's creation. The newborn reflects some of the parents' physical characteristics, and soon learns to mimic their words and gestures.

Imagine the pain and grief in the heart of any mother who is forced to give up her baby! After carrying her child in her womb for nine months, giving birth, feeding her baby at her breast, and cuddling the infant close to her heart, how could she bear to let that baby go? Well, that's exactly what Jochebed, the mother of Moses, faced only three months after his birth.

Fathers, I want to use this example of the sacrifice of Moses's parents to illustrate that it is God who gives us our children, and it is God who can also ask us to release them to Him for His purposes.

Let us examine the context of this story that is recorded in the first two chapters of Exodus.

Pharaoh had issued a cruel edict that all the Jewish baby boys born in Egypt had to be killed by being thrown into the crocodile-infested waters of the Nile River. The intent was to reduce the population of the Jewish people, who were slaves in Egypt, the world power at that time.

However, God had other plans for the third-born child of this humble Jewish family. One day this little baby would become one of the greatest leaders of Israel—after his forty-year preparation in Pharaoh's palace and an additional forty-year training period in the desert.

God has a plan for each of us to accomplish, and we, as parents, need to trust God and allow Him to fulfill His plan. At times, this will require sacrifice on our part. The parents of Moses trusted God with their newborn son. It was because of that trust in God that they did not allow their son to be killed. They sensed he was an unusual child whom God would use greatly one day, so they found a creative way to fulfill the letter of Pharaoh's law, while at the same time preserving the baby's life. They placed baby Moses in a waterproofed covered basket, and then they placed the basket among the reeds in the Nile River.

You know the story. Pharaoh's daughter came to the river to bathe, and she heard the baby's cries. Her heart was touched by this tragic situation, and she decided to adopt the infant and raise him as her own. *But who will nurse this newborn?* she thought. Just then, Moses's older sister, Miriam, ran up and offered to have her mother nurse the baby.

What was the result of Jochebed letting go and giving her helpless infant into the Lord's care? She received her child back again, and was even paid to care for him!

We are not told how long Jochebed was allowed to be with her biological son, but it is quite possible that she remained his nanny for a long period of time—so long that Moses, as a grown man, would identify himself as Jewish and not as the son of the daughter of Pharaoh.

The mother of Moses did all this **by faith**. The Bible says, "[God] is a rewarder of those who diligently seek Him" (Hebrews 11:6 NKJV). When we release our children to God, He not only blesses them, but we also receive a reward that is greater than we could ever expect. It is a principle that governs all of heaven.

Every Christian can quote John 3:16, but the deeper truth of that passage is that we can have eternal life because God, our Father, gave us His only Son! He released Jesus to not only be born with a human body, but to grow up in a human family and to one day fulfill a very difficult and painful task—to die for us sinful humans.

Stop and consider this: There is no resurrection until there is a death. There is no receiving something back until it is truly given up. There is no reward until there is surrender. Our heavenly Father showed us this principle with His Son, Jesus. He gave Him up for **us**!

Did you ever stop to think that your beloved children are **not really yours**, but are given to you by God for a purpose? This means that our children belong to **Him**. He only lends them to us for a time so that we can raise them, teach them about God, and then release them for whatever purpose God has for them. I wish more parents would realize this simple truth.

Sadly, many parents take a selfish approach with their children. They insist that their children live near them so they can continue to influence the decisions that their grown children make. Even after their children marry and have children of their own, these parents want to continue to exercise their authority over them.

The apostle Paul says that this approach is wrong. Children are not for the parents, but parents are for the children (2 Corinthians 12:14). Although the context of that verse refers to saving up an inheritance for our children, it also refers to the broader concept of who gives what to whom. In other words, our goal as parents is to help our children become more successful than we are. That includes **releasing** them to the calling that they have been given by God, not holding on to the one that we desire for them.

Here is another very important principle that parents should observe: When our children reach adulthood, they shift from being under our chain of command to being alongside us as we offer our counsel. This is a huge difference. Children should never lose respect for or stop honoring their parents, but parents of grown children need to understand that there is a time to **release** their children from their command and control so they can make their own decisions in life.

It is true that this is one of the most difficult times of our lives. This was true for my wife and me, and it was also difficult for our children to see one of their siblings leave home for the first time.

This happened when our oldest son, AJ, left for college two hours away from our home in Charlotte. We gathered in the kitchen and held hands as the time to drive him away to school approached. It was a tearful time for all of us, but I noticed that AJ's younger brother, Luke, was especially affected. Up until this time, AJ and Luke had rarely been apart. They had always done everything together, whether driving to high school, playing sports, or attending church activities. They even shared a bedroom with twin beds when they could have had their own room. They chose to sleep in the same bedroom.

I could see Luke's tears as AJ said goodbye, and I felt how deeply Luke loved his older brother. Letting go is hard, even for the kids. Before I tell you how Esty and I said our farewells later that day on AJ's campus, let me first tell you what I felt I had to do for Luke when we returned home.

There was no way I could have him sleep in the same bedroom where his brother used to be and have Luke stare at his empty bed. No. We sold the twin beds, bought a larger bed for Luke, and turned his former bedroom into the upstairs family room.

We then took the upstairs office and converted it into Luke's new private bedroom. We painted the walls a Carolina-blue color and set him up with new furniture. A new chapter in our family life had begun. Having his new room did much to heal his heart as he missed his big brother. We all missed his big brother!

When we dropped AJ off at his university two hours away from home, I had a whole list of "don'ts" that I wanted to tell him: "Don't sin, don't do drugs, don't commit immorality, don't get drunk and hang out with bad guys—don't, don't, don't!"

Sometimes I think we want to say these things more for our own sake because it makes **us** feel better that we warned them sufficiently!

As we prepared to say goodbye, the Holy Spirit whispered to my heart: "Don't tell him any of those things. He already knows not to do them."

*So, then, what **do** I tell him?* I thought.

The response came swiftly to my heart: "Tell him that you trust him and that you believe he will do the right thing."

I looked my firstborn son in the eye and, instead of all the "don'ts" running through my mind, I said this: "AJ, we have raised you to grow wings. Now lift up those wings and fly for Jesus. I trust you and believe in you."

His eyes welled up with tears, and I will never forget his next words: "Thank you, Dad, for your trust in me. I will not let you down." And he didn't.

He had a successful four years at that university. He excelled in academics and athletics, and he met his wife, Whitney, in a Christian club on campus for athletes. He went on to medical school in North Carolina, followed by residency in Florida, and he now has a successful practice as a surgeon in Orlando. He and Whitney have two children—our first grandchild, Adelaide, and a son named Graham.

A few years later, it was even more difficult for us, as we had to say goodbye to our second son, Luke. His university was fourteen hours away in Missouri. We could travel the two hours to visit AJ fairly easily, but we knew it would be much harder to visit Luke.

After registering him at the school, we stopped at Andy's Frozen Custard to say our goodbyes. I can't remember ever crying so hard as when we drove away and left him that day in God's care. Letting go is truly hard. We know this by experience.

Luke also excelled in academics and sports and had favor with his teachers and coach. A few summers later, Luke went with me to a speaking engagement I had at a family camp in Santa Cruz, California, where we met a wonderful Christian girl, also named Whitney, from that area. Luke and Whitney eventually got married in the Bay Area, and Luke finished his graduate degree in Pasadena, California.

Luke now has a doctorate and serves our country as an officer in the US Air Force. He is a trained psychologist, ministering to airmen who struggle with difficulties such as PTSD and alcohol and drug abuse, as well as ministering in the area of suicide prevention. He and Whitney are now stationed near Macon, Georgia. They have three children—two girls, Harper and Stella, and a boy, Tatum.

When it was Larissa's turn, she chose to go to the same college as Luke, which made it so much easier for us to visit both of them. They even shared an apartment together for a time in Springfield, Missouri.

As it turned out, Larissa fell in love with a great Christian guy named Isaac, and their wedding was held in Branson, Missouri. We wanted to live near at least one of our children, and circumstances led us to Ozark, Missouri, where we presently live near our daughter and son-in-law and their three children—a boy, Canon, and two girls, Aspen and Mila.

Both of our sons have earned doctorates and enjoy successful careers. My daughter has a teaching degree, and she taught in a charter school before she had children. The time our children spent doing homework and learning discipline in their work has brought wonderful success to their lives.

My children may not be in the ministry in the same way that I am, but they all minister to the physical and emotional hurts of people in places and in ways I could never have access to. It is evident to me that God had a specific plan for each of my children, and I am certain that He has one for each of your children as well.

We are now grandparents who love to visit our grown children and grandkids, but it is important to point out that whenever my wife and I visit any of our three grown children's homes, we honor **their rules** and procedures. When we sit around their dinner table, I wait for my sons or daughter to indicate who will pray for the meal. **Their house, their rules.** Honor their authority while in their homes, and that, in turn, teaches their children that respect is rendered in both directions.

If you truly believe that God wants to bless and use your children, then trust His guidance and release them to His care, as the mother of Moses did. Your greatest reward will be to see the wonderful future God has for them unfold before your eyes.

CHAPTER 18:

Returning Home

In My Father's house . . .
John 14:12 NKJV

"In My Father's house." What did Jesus mean when He said those words? Does God actually live in a house?

With this phrase, "My Father's house," Jesus reveals a few powerful truths.

Jesus is calling God His Father. This "house" that He is referring to is actually in heaven; it belongs to His Father, and it is a place where Jesus wants us to live.

Up until Jesus, no one had ever referred to God as Father. It was quite a shocking statement for the Jewish religious leaders of the time to hear. Just think about it: Yahweh, the Creator God who formed the sun, moon, and stars just by speaking; the all-powerful God who shook Mount Sinai with a mighty earthquake, lightning flashes, and crashing thunder; God, the Righteous Lawgiver who wrote the Ten Commandments on stone tablets with His finger—Jesus calls Him Father! You can see how this might be confusing for the religious leaders.

Jesus reassured His troubled disciples that His Father does indeed have a house, a dwelling place, for a specific purpose. He wants us to live **with Him** for the rest of eternity: "I am going to prepare a place for you," Jesus said. "When everything is ready, I will come and get you, so that **you will always be with me** where I am" (John 14:2–3 NLT).

It is not just the house that comforted the disciples, but they were also comforted by the fact that Jesus promised to live with them forever in that house. It is a theme that the Scriptures return to again and again: God desires to have an eternal relationship with us, His creation.

Much later, the apostle John was given a vision of this future dwelling place. Revelation 21 records what he saw and heard:

> And I saw the holy city, new Jerusalem, coming down out of heaven from God. . . . And I heard a loud voice from the throne saying: "Behold, the dwelling place of God is with man. **He will dwell with them**, and they will be his people, and **God himself will be with them as their God**. He will wipe away every tear from their eyes." (Revelation 21:2–4 ESV)

From the very creation of man, recorded in the book of Genesis, to this last written chapter of man's history in Revelation, it has always been God's desire to live together with us. In the garden of Eden, the Lord God would walk with Adam and Eve in the coolness of the evening, each and every day.

In the desert wilderness, God led His people with a pillar of cloud by day and with fire by night—a literal manifestation of His presence. Whenever the pillar stopped, the people made preparations to make camp there. In the middle of the camp, a tabernacle was set up where the glory of God rested above the ark of the covenant.

The twelve tribes of Israel would surround the tabernacle, with three tribes facing in toward the center of each of the four sides of the compass. Situated right in the middle of the twelve tribes of Israel was the actual presence of the Shekinah, the glory of God, in the inner room of the tabernacle. What a way for God to demonstrate that He wanted to be in the midst of His people!

In Bethlehem, the angels rejoiced at the birth of Jesus, joyously celebrating that this magnificent God took on a mortal body and was born into the humble family of a carpenter and his wife. Jesus did all this to be among us, to love us, and to reveal His Father in heaven to us. At the same time, in Joseph and Mary's home, He experienced what it was like to grow up in a family.

With this historical background in mind, I believe that Jesus comforted His disciples about their future home in heaven because a home, the place in which we live, has such a powerful influence on our lives. Home is family; Dad and Mom are always near to us. Home is where our most impressionable memories were created, where we smelled the rich aroma of borsch that Mom was stirring on the stove. Home is where we gathered around the table and where Dad led us in prayer before so many delicious meals.

It is significant that the very first organized activity at the end of time, at the beginning of eternity in the next life, will be a celebration dinner. Jesus will sit down with us at an enormous table to celebrate the beginning of eternity. He Himself extends the invitation to us: "'Come, for all things are now ready'" (Luke 14:17 NKJV).

There is a place setting there for you, dear friend, and you are invited to sit at His table in our Father's house.

Have you ever truly given your heart to God? Like the prodigal son, we have all sinned and gone astray in our selfishness, but the heavenly Father waits for us to return to Him so He can restore us to our rightful place at His table. The prodigal son realized that he had to acknowledge and confess his foolish choices before he could enter his father's home again. His words, just before he got up and left the pig pen, were, "I will arise and go to my father, and I will say to him, 'Father, I have sinned against heaven and before you'" (Luke 15:18 ESV).

Say those words to God. Truly mean them from

your heart. This involves leaving your sin behind and returning to your heavenly Father. He is waiting for you with open arms of forgiveness. Know this: great joy and celebration follow your return home to Him!

ABOUT THE AUTHOR

George Davidiuk was born in New Jersey of Ukrainian immigrant parents. He's a favorite speaker of teens and adults with a teaching ministry that takes him around the world. He has traveled extensively to the former countries of the Soviet Union, having visited them over 100 times since 1973. He and his wife Esty presently live in Ozark, Missouri. They have three married children and eight grandchildren.

ACKNOWLEDGEMENTS

First and foremost, I want to thank my wife of nearly 40 years for her support and encouragement for me to write this book. As I wrote about my participation as a father in raising our three children, it might seem like I did a lot of the heavy lifting. Nothing is further from the truth! My wife is an amazing mother who nursed all her children, cooked all the meals, kept our house incredibly clean and orderly, organized our school schedules and sports activities, and was active in the PTA. She managed all these things while she was working as a nurse and I had to travel overseas for ministry. The book focused more on what my role was in order to encourage other men to be more active fathers and participate in raising their children more than just providing the finances to their home. Esty, you are my inspiration!

Next, I would like to acknowledge Esther Fedd for her skill, vision, and expertise to get this project rolling. She, together with her talented husband Jimmy, have contributed so much to bring my ministry to fruition, both in recorded music and now in book form! God has truly used both of you to bless many, many others! Thank you!

It was my delight to meet and work closely with the amazing staff at Fedd Agency, Allison East who so graciously worked closely with me to ensure the artwork, fonts, and cover were first class! I enjoyed working with you! I also want to thank Tori Thacher for her skill in editing the manuscript with Allison Harrell, and the rest of the staff, Danielle, Ginny, and Kyle. The office staff was so professional and amazing! Glad to work with you!

Finally, I want to acknowledge my Dad, Andrew Davidiuk, whose prayers throughout my childhood protected me from evil, guided me through life, and showed me the best of example of a kind and loving father who blessed his home! You left us an incredible legacy that I pray we can also leave for our children and grandchildren!

There are certain ones that I also truly want to thank. They gave such a generous gift that made this first printing possible. God knows who you are and the reward from heaven is so much better than my mentioning your name. But I thank you for your faithfulness to our ministry.

George Davidiuk
Ozark, MO

AJ, Whitney, Adelaide, and Graham

Luke, Whitney, Harper, Stella, and Tatum

Larissa, Isaac, Canon, Aspen, and Mila

George and his father, Andrew Davidiuk

The Davidiuk Kids

ENDNOTES

1 James C. Dobson, *New Dare to Discipline* (Carol Stream, IL: Tyndale House, 2014), 27-28, 36.

2 Liraz Margalit, "What Screen Time Can Really Do to Kids' Brains," *Psychology Today*, April 17, 2016, https://www.psychologytoday.com/us/blog/behind-online-behavior/201604/what-screen-time-can-really-do-kids-brains.

3 "Part 1—Benefits of Chores," The Center for Parenting Education, accessed August 26, 2020, https://centerforparentingeducation.org/library-of-articles/responsibility-and-chores/part-i-benefits-of-chores.

4 Weinstein, Edie. "Do Chores Teach Children Responsibility?" Psych Central, October 8, 2018. https://psychcentral.com/lib/do-chores-teach-children-responsibility/.

5 Scientific information about pornography is taken from the following articles:

Kyle K. Pitchers, Vincent Vialou, Eric J. Nestler, Steven R. Laviolette, Michael N. Lehman, and Lique M. Coolen, "Natural and Drug Rewards Act on Common Neural Plasticity Mechanisms with DeltaFosB as a Key Mediator," *Journal of Neuroscience* (February 20, 2013).

Donald L. Hilton Jr., "Pornography Addiction—A Supranormal Stimulus Considered in the Context of Neuroplasticity," *Journal of*

Neuroscience (July 19, 2013).

Donald L. Hilton and Clark Watts, "Pornography Addiction: A Neuroscience Perspective" *Surgical Neurology International*, (February 21, 2011), http://www.ncbi.nlm.nih.gov/pmc/articles/PMC3050060.

6   Chapman, Gary D. The 5 Love Languages. Chicago: Northfield Pub., 2015.

7   Helen Doron, "30 Phrases for Encouraging Someone in English," HelenDoron.com, accessed August 26, 2020, https://www.helendoron.com/30-phrases-for-encouraging-someone-in-english.

8   Field, T. "American adolescents touch each other less and are more aggressive toward their peers as compared with French adolescents." Adolescence (1999): 753-758.

9   Dutton, Julie, Ashleigh Johnson, and Mark Hickson. "Touch Revisited: Observations and Methodological Recommendations." Journal of Mass Communication & Journalism 07, no. 05 (2017). https://doi.org/10.4172/2165-7912.1000348.

10   George Howe Colt and Anne Hollister, "Discovery: The Magic of Touch Massage's Healing Powers Make It Serious Medicine." *Life*, August 1997, 52.

11   John Martin, "21. Rings on his fingers," https://prodigalprof.com/the-prodigal/21-rings-on-his-fingers/.